CHINA

lenovo联想
联想 乐Pad
平板电脑
带上乐Pad去旅行
乐自由我
井冈山饭店
井冈山饭店 JINGGANG
井冈山邮政速递物流
-11183
商务酒店
杂品商店

ANHOTEL
祝江西省第十一次急诊医学学术会议圆满成功
热烈欢迎太原市检察机关领导干部素能培训班的各位学员!
老蔡
电话 0796-6557818

12

NO:05

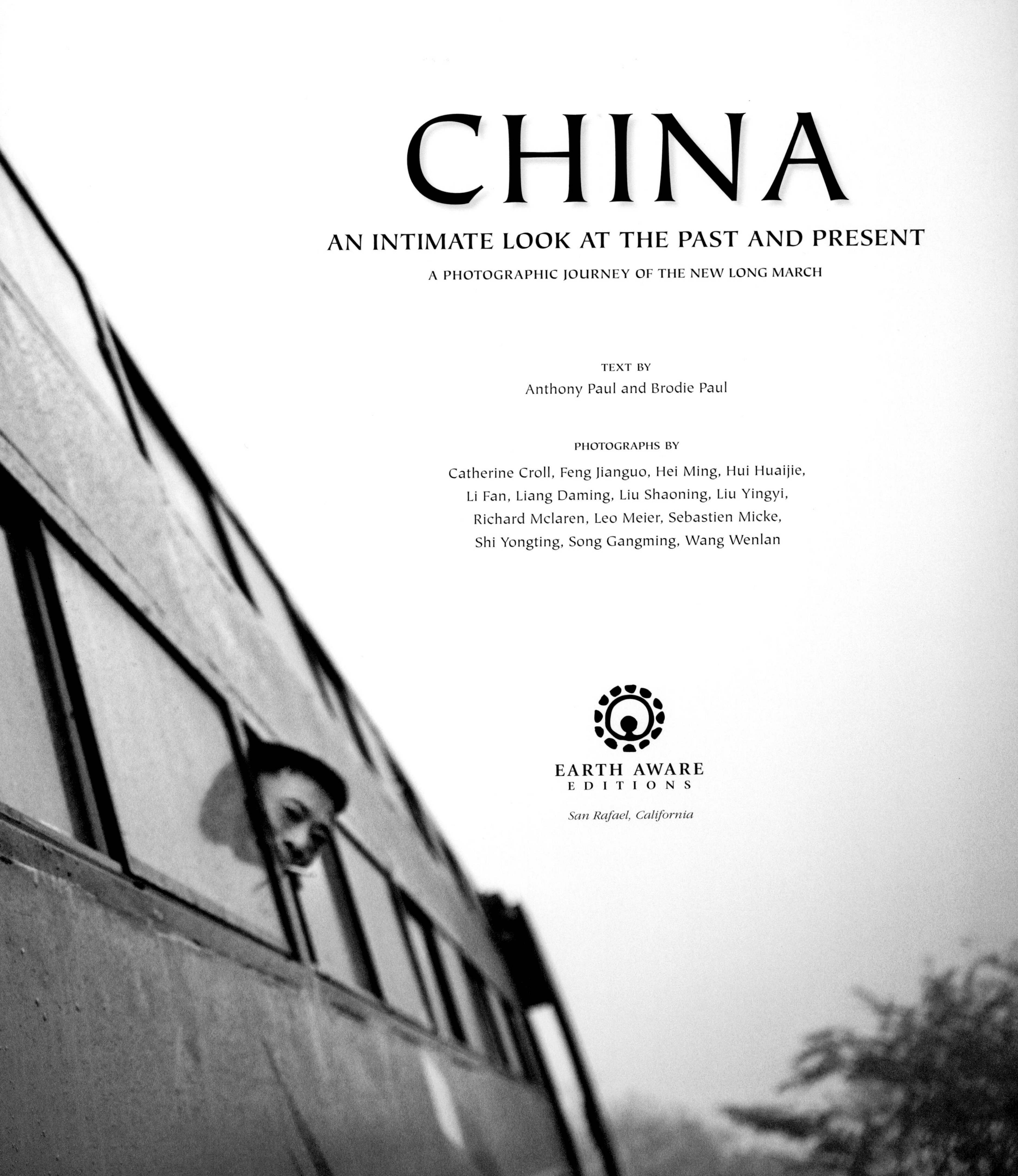

CHINA

AN INTIMATE LOOK AT THE PAST AND PRESENT

A PHOTOGRAPHIC JOURNEY OF THE NEW LONG MARCH

TEXT BY

Anthony Paul and Brodie Paul

PHOTOGRAPHS BY

Catherine Croll, Feng Jianguo, Hei Ming, Hui Huaijie, Li Fan, Liang Daming, Liu Shaoning, Liu Yingyi, Richard Mclaren, Leo Meier, Sebastien Micke, Shi Yongting, Song Gangming, Wang Wenlan

EARTH AWARE EDITIONS

San Rafael, California

EARTH AWARE
EDITIONS

PO Box 3088, San Rafael, CA 94912
www.earthawareeditions.com

First published in the United States in 2012 by Earth Aware Editions, an imprint of Insight Editions

Library of Congress Cataloging-in-Publication Data available.
ISBN: 978-1-60887-150-6

Insight Editions, in association with Roots of Peace, will plant two trees for each tree used in the manufacturing of this book. Roots of Peace is an internationally renowned humanitarian organization dedicated to eradicating land mines worldwide and converting war-torn lands into productive farms and wildlife habitats. Together, we will plant two million fruit and nut trees in Afghanistan and provide farmers there with the skills and support necessary for sustainable land use.

Prepress by Splitting Image, Melbourne, Australia
Printed in China by 1010 Printing International Limited.

10 9 8 7 6 5 4 3 2 1

The Red Seals

The red seals, known colloquially in Asia as chops, that appear at the beginning of each chapter were specially commissioned for this book. In Chapters 1 to 7 they say "The Long March to Victory" and in Chapters 8 to 13 they say "The Long March Continues."

Note On Pronunciation

Chinese names in *China: An Intimate Look at the Past and Present* are spelled according to the Pinyin system. Names written in Pinyin are usually pronounced more or less as written, but there are some important exceptions:

c is pronounced as *ts* (Cao is pronounced *Tsao*)
q is pronounced as *ch* (Qing Dynasty is pronounced *Ching Dynasty*)
x is pronounced as *s* (Xiang River is pronounced *Siang River*)
z is pronounced as *dz* (Mao Zedong is pronounced *Mao Dzedong*)
zh is pronounced as *j* (Zhou Enlai is pronounced *Jou Enlai*)

We have not followed Pinyin in cases where an earlier form is so well known that changes would tend to confuse. We have therefore kept the names of Sun Yat-sen and Chiang Kai-shek for the English-language edition.

Produced by

Qingdao Publishing House,
182 Haier Road, Qingdao China P.C 266061
www.qdpub.com
and
Weldon International Pty Ltd,
GPO Box 5390, Sydney NSW 2001, Australia
A MEMBER OF THE WELDON MEDIA GROUP
www.weldonmedia.com

Qingdao Publishing House
Publisher Meng Mingfei
Editors-in-Charge Gao Jimin, Liu Yong, Shen Yao
Cover Concept Design Center, Qingdao Publishing House

Weldon Global (Beijing)
Project Directors Harold Weldon, Li Dong
Project Coordinator Shen Wei
Chinese Translation Li Yao

Weldon International
Publishing Director Elaine Russell
Creative Director Leonie Weldon
Project Editor Peter Dockrill
Design Concept Jacqueline Richards
Designers Jacqueline Richards, Alex Frampton
Picture Editors Leonie Weldon, Catherine Croll, Jude Fowler Smith, Tony Gordon, Leo Meier
Digital Asset Management Leo Meier
Cartography Laurie Whiddon
Calligraphy Deng Shaomin
Proofreader Kevin Diletti
Index Diane Harriman
Production Tony Gordon

Photographers
Catherine Croll, Australia; Feng Jianguo, China; Hei Ming, China; Hui Huaijie, China; Li Fan, China; Liang Daming, China; Liu Shaoning, China; Liu Yingyi, China; Richard Mclaren, United Kingdom/USA; Leo Meier, Switzerland/Australia; Sebastien Micke, France/USA; Shi Yongting, China ; Song Gangming, China ; Wang Wenlan, China
Survey Trip Michael Young, Australia

Authors
Anthony Paul and Brodie Paul
Additional Text and Captions Harold Weldon, Peter Dockrill

Digital Feature: Images, Videos and Songs
This Weldon Media Group digital innovation feature appears on page 393

To access this feature, visit www.longmarchbook.com

A WELDON GLOBAL (BEIJING) INITIATIVE

FRONT COVER (top) Mountains in Danba County, Sichuan province LI FAN; (bottom) Red Army soliders cross a river on pontoons, a common technique during the Long March and in later campaigns. PEOPLE'S LIBERATION ARMY PHOTO ARCHIVE

FRONT ENDPAPER "Poetry of the Long March" ZHANG FENGTANG

PAGES 2–3 Danba County, Sichuan province LI FAN

PAGES 4–5 "Red Tourists" wearing replica Red Army uniforms to evoke the spirit of the Red Army, Ci Ping, Jiangangshan, Jiangxi province LIU SHAONING

PAGES 6–7 Longji (Dragon's Backbone) Rice Terraces, Longsheng, Guangxi Zhuang Autonomous Region LIU YINGYI

PAGES 8–9 Ethnic Naxi villagers, Lugu Lake, Sichuan province WANG WENLAN

TITLE PAGE On the road to Luding, Sichuan province LIANG DAMING

OPPOSITE Cave house, Ansai, Shaanxi province SONG GANGMING

CONTENTS Shaanxi Cultural Performance Troupe, Ansai, Shaanxi province MICHAEL YOUNG

PAGE 18 Mahjongg player, Xiaojin county, Sichuan province RICHARD MCLAREN

PAGES 20–21 Half Moon River Bend, Hongyuan, Hongyuan–Rou'ergai Grassland, Sichuan province LEO MEIER

BACK ENDPAPER "Poetry of Liu Pan Shan (mountain)" ZHANG FENGTANG

春
紅太陽
福
紅日東升山
東風浩蕩氣象
ROVA
乐华彩电
智能电视

Contents

[illegible]長酒

In Their Footsteps

The history of the world is marked by great moments of human achievement, of epic triumph against all odds. China's Long March was such an event—a 6,000-mile (10,000-kilometer) journey through hazardous terrain across the length and breadth of China by the men and women of the Red Army. It was an odyssey, without parallel in modern history, that ended in victory.

China: An Intimate Look at the Past and Present revisits the areas where that momentous journey took place. A dramatic portrait of ordinary people, breathtaking landscapes and the all-encompassing energy that can be found all along the route today is shown through the eyes of some of the world's great photographers.

In 1985, I retraced the Long March route as part of the team that produced the book *China: The Long March* celebrating the 50th anniversary of the Long March. Twenty-six years later, I once again journeyed along the route on the survey trip for the images in this book. The Team Leader of the survey trip was Li Dong, who was also a member of the original team and is now my business partner.

We witnessed a country undergoing great transformation, with roads, rail lines, bridges and tunnels under construction across the thousands of miles of our travels. Small villages had become towns and towns had become cities. Everywhere people were active, busily working on their own New Long March.

As an Australian I am honored that my Chinese colleagues have invited me to share in their history and to help tell their stories to the world. All along the Long March route, the spirit of the local people, as they work to build better lives for themselves and their children, continues to give meaning to the sacrifice and struggle of the Red Army in 1934–36.

This book is an historic publishing venture between Qingdao Publishing Group and Weldon International. It is a testimony to the 26 years of mutual friendship and respect that has grown since I first visited China. It has been an exciting journey to personally experience the compelling spirit of the Long March as it lives on in China today.

Harold Weldon

Introduction

China's history is full of surprises and unexpected turns, and perhaps the greatest of them all was the Long March. When the Red Army began its retreat across China in October 1934, the future of the Communist uprising looked bleak. How could an 80,000-strong peasant army with largely homemade arms withstand the Nationalist force of 900,000 men led by experienced generals and equipped with the latest weapons?

But the Red Army, under Mao Zedong's leadership, somehow survived its two-year trek across the mountains, snowfields, bogs and deserts of some of Asia's most unforgiving terrain. Certain defeat was transformed into a galvanizing tale of survival, endurance and comradeship. The Long March became one of the turning points in modern Chinese history, setting the stage for the creation of the People's Republic of China in 1949.

China: An Intimate Look at the Past and Present is a celebration of that spirit, 75 years on. In late 2011 we sent a team of Chinese and international photographers along the route of the original Long March—from Jiangxi in the southeast to Gansu and Shaanxi in the northwest. The breathtaking, insightful and beautiful images they brought back reveal a land, and a people, that have undergone change of almost unbelievable proportions. Villages have become cities and towns have become megacities. Dirt tracks have been transformed into superhighways, and rivers have been harnessed by massive hydroelectric projects. And everywhere the buzz of industry and commerce fills the air.

But underneath it all, a deep feeling of pride, determination and perseverance—the same spirit that turned the Long March from a disaster into a triumph—can be found throughout this region. As you turn the pages of *China: An Intimate Look at the Past and Present*, you'll see it in the faces of ordinary people, first among the soldiers in the historical images of the Long March, and then among the men, women and children who bring so much joy, energy and life to the amazing new photographs of the region today.

A commemorative reliving of the Red Army's epoch-making trek, *China: An Intimate Look at the Past and Present* takes readers to where history is still being made. Shortly before final victory in the Communist revolution in 1949, Mao declared, "We are not only good at breaking up an old world, we will also be good at creating a new one." Perhaps even the Great Helmsman himself would be surprised to see how true his words have proven to be.

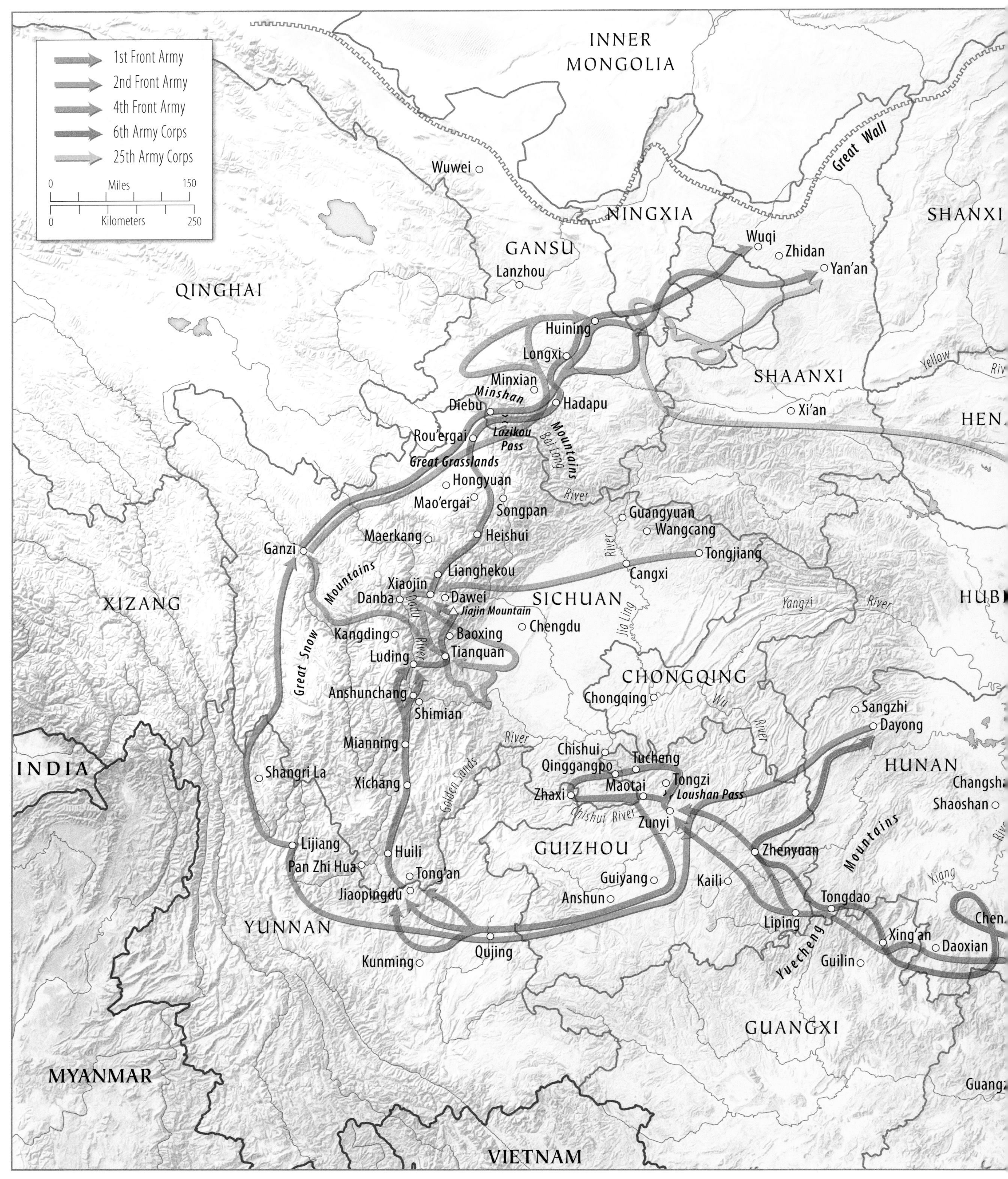
1st Front Army
2nd Front Army
4th Front Army
6th Army Corps
25th Army Corps
0 Miles 150
0 Kilometers 250
INNER MONGOLIA
NINGXIA
SHANXI
GANSU
QINGHAI
SHAANXI
SICHUAN
XIZANG
CHONGQING
HUNAN
GUIZHOU
YUNNAN
GUANGXI
INDIA
MYANMAR
VIETNAM
Great Wall
Wuwei
Wuqi
Zhidan
Yan'an
Lanzhou
Huining
Longxi
Minxian
Minshan
Diebu
Hadapu
Lazikou Pass
Mountains
Bai Long River
Rou'ergai
Great Grasslands
Hongyuan
Mao'ergai
Songpan
Xi'an
Yellow River
Guangyuan
Wangcang
Tongjiang
Cangxi
Maerkang
Heishui
Ganzi
Lianghekou
Xiaojin
Danba
Dawei
Jiajin Mountain
Kangding
Baoxing
Chengdu
Luding
Tianquan
Dadu River
Jia Ling River
Yangzi River
Great Snow Mountains
Anshunchang
Shimian
Chongqing
Wu River
Sangzhi
Dayong
Mianning
Chishui
Tucheng
Qinggangpo
Tongzi
Maotai
Loushan Pass
Zhaxi
Zunyi
Chishui River
Xichang
Shangri La
Golden Sands River
Lijiang
Pan Zhi Hua
Huili
Tong'an
Jiaopingdu
Guiyang
Anshun
Kaili
Zhenyuan
Mountains
Xiang
Tongdao
Liping
Yuecheng
Xing'an
Daoxian
Guilin
Qujing
Kunming
Changsha
Shaoshan
HUB
HEN
Chen
Guang

The Long March

1934

OCT 16 Long March begins as first Red Army units cross the Yudu River. In all, 86,000 troops are on the move.

NOV 25–DEC 1 Battle of Xiang River. An estimated 30,000 Red Army soldiers are killed or wounded, or desert.

1935

JAN 15–17 Zunyi Conference. Politburo and military leaders debate setbacks. Meeting supports Mao, whose faction is now dominant. New plan directs Red Army to move north across Yangzi River.

JAN 28 Battle of Qinggangpo. After suffering heavy losses, Red Army retreats west across Chishui River.

FEB 5 First Zhaxi Meeting. Mao supporter Zhang Wentian replaces Bo Gu as senior Communist Party leader.

FEB 7 Second Zhaxi Meeting. Plan to cross Yangzi canceled.

FEB 10 Third Zhaxi Meeting. Red Army directed to re-cross Chishui River and return to Zunyi.

FEB 28 Red Army wins first major victory of the Long March as Zunyi is retaken.

MAR 21–22 Final crossing of Chishui River.

APR 29 Red Army feigns attack on Kunming. Panic grips city.

MAY 8 Red Army completes crossing of Golden Sands River. Trek north across Sichuan begins.

MAY 22 Liu Bocheng seals Red Army alliance with Yi minority.

MAY 29 Red Army wins battle of Luding Bridge, allowing troops to cross the Dadu River.

JUN 12–16 First Front Army crosses the Great Snow Mountains and finds Zhang Guotao's Fourth Front Army. Combined force has more than 100,000 soldiers.

AUG 21 Crossing of Great Grasslands begins.

SEP 10 Combined First Front–Fourth Front Army splits. Mao leads his force north; Zhang Guotao turns south and re-crosses Great Grasslands.

SEP 15–16 Battle of Lazikou. First Front Army crosses Minshan range and leaves Tibetan region. Fewer than 10,000 men left.

SEP 21 First Front Army soldiers find newspapers in Hadapu confirming that Red Army troops are active in northwest Shaanxi province.

OCT 19 The First Front Army reaches Wuqi, ending their Long March. Approximately 4,000 survivors.

1936

APR 25–28 Second Front Army under He Long and Ren Bishi crosses the Yangzi River, Yunnan province, and marches north toward Xizang.

AUG Zhang Guotao's Fourth Front Army suffers massive casualties in running battles with troops of GMD-allied warlord Ma Bufang.

OCT 22 Second Front Army and Fourth Front Army join up with First Front Army in Huining, officially bringing the Long March to an end.

THE LONG MARCH TO VICTORY

CHAPTER 1

Turbulent Times

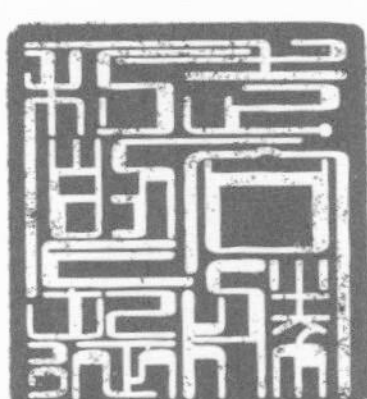

As the 19th century became the 20th, China was in a shambles. The Qing dynasty had ruled the country for more than 250 years. For more than 50 years armies from distant lands—Britain, France, Germany, Austria, Italy, Russia—intervened almost at will in China's political affairs and commerce.

In a war sponsored by British opium smugglers and backed by the Royal Navy, Britain seized Hong Kong and some of China's finest ports, including Shanghai. When patriotic Chinese forces responded by attacking Christian missionaries, Western armies invaded. At one point, Westerners shelled and looted the Summer Palace, a treasured area of elegant structures outside the capital.

Weakened by these humiliations, a succession of emperors gradually lost their control over China, especially in the more distant provinces. In many of these areas warlords—bandit generals—ruled, their opulent lives financed by plunder from some of the world's most wretched peasants.

LEFT The Nanchang Uprising, which began on August 1, 1927, was the first major engagement between Communist and Nationalist forces. Today August 1 is seen as the foundation day of the Red Army. This painting shows Zhou Enlai rallying Communist troops on the steps of the Nanchang council building.

XINHUA NEWS AGENCY

LEFT Sun Yat-sen, seen here with his wife Soong Ching-ling, became China's first president in 1912. Today he is revered as the 'Forerunner of the Revolution' in mainland China.
CHINA FOTOPRESS

Ravaged by warlord armies of often-unspeakable cruelty, plague, starvation and natural disasters, most farmers faced a life of unceasing misery. The country was ready for dramatic change.

After millennia of rule by emperors who claimed to enjoy the Mandate of Heaven, notions of republican government began to take hold. At the forefront of this gathering revolution emerged an unlikely leader, Dr. Sun Yat-sen. With the appearance and manner of the Christian missionaries who had educated him, this middle-aged physician had never held political or administrative office.

Obsessed by a vision of a New China, Sun traveled the world as an increasingly popular, anti-Manchu revolutionary. He spoke passionately to exiled students about what could be possible if China drove its corrupt rulers from power and built a democratic republic.

Sun formed the Revive China Party based on three principles: nationalism, democracy and the "people's livelihood." This last notion held that every Chinese was entitled to a fair share of food, clothing, housing and education.

Talk turned into armed uprising in Wuchang, a Yangzi River district, on October 10, 1911. Fighting quickly spread to Nanjing, where republican forces defeated Manchu troops. Sun, who had been fundraising in North America and Europe, hurried home. When revolutionaries seized power in major cities, he was elected president of the newly formed Chinese Republic in December 1911.

The last emperor, six-year-old Pu Yi, abdicated several weeks later. The following August, the Revive China Party merged with other revolutionary groups to form the Chinese Nationalist Party (Guomindang or GMD) with Sun as leader.

But Sun's dreams of a strong republican administration were not to be. A weak provisional government that was often beholden to warlords ruled a politically fragmented nation. The ongoing chaos attracted the attention of an increasingly powerful, expansionist military in neighboring Japan.

At the time, China's other great neighbor, Russia, was undergoing its own revolution. In 1917, disaffected Russian students, workers and troops rose up under the leadership of Vladimir Lenin, a devotee of Karl Marx's theories of class struggle and governance. The Czar was overthrown and eventually murdered. The aristocrats and capitalists who had long ruled Russia were either killed or driven into exile, replaced by a new political and economic order—the Union of Soviet Socialist Republics.

The USSR's central authority was the Communist Party. Like most first-generation revolutionaries, Soviet Communists displayed Messianic, near-religious tendencies—their revolution should be spread throughout the world. They created the Communist International (Comintern) to help Marx's followers replicate the Russian experience worldwide.

Young we were, schoolmates,
At life's full flowering; filled with student enthusiasm,
Boldly we cast all restraints aside.
Pointing to our mountains and rivers,
Setting people afire with our words,
We counted the mighty no more than muck.

Excerpt from the 1925 poem Changsha, by Mao Zedong

"Since the overthrow of the Qing dynasty, we have carried out only one part of our obligations: we have fulfilled only our passive duty, but have done nothing in the realm of positive work," Sun Yat-sen declared in 1921. "We must raise the prestige of the Chinese people, and unite all the races inhabiting China to form one Chinese people in eastern Asia, a Chinese national state."

ABOVE The soviets created by the Communists in the 1920s and '30s were fledgling states, complete with their own currency. This bank note, featuring the face of Lenin, was issued by the soviet of the Fourth Front Army in northeast Sichuan.
PAUL LAU

China's Marxists were then a scattering of mostly students browsing in libraries or gathering in teashops to discuss news from Russia. After a group of them approached Moscow for help and funds, Comintern executive Hendricus Sneevliet was sent to Shanghai in June 1921. Not everyone was impressed by the Dutchman, who had spent five years advising the Communist Party of the Dutch East Indies (now Indonesia). "He had acquired the habits and attitudes of the Dutchmen that lived as colonial masters," noted Zhang Guotao, a Marxist activist.

But Sneevliet's arrival was useful to the would-be revolutionaries. In Shanghai

13 delegates from Communist groups gathered to meet him and attend the founding Congress of the Chinese Communist Party (CCP) in July 1921. They included Mao Zedong, a 28-year-old Hunan-born library assistant who had moved to Shanghai and was making a living by taking in laundry.

They met in a girls' boarding school in Shanghai's French quarter that had been closed for the summer holidays.

ABOVE Many young Chinese revolutionaries went to Europe to study. This group of young Communists, photographed in Paris in 1924, included future Chinese premier Zhou Enlai (front row, fouth from left).
CHINA FOTOPRESS

The party's first formal statement called for the formation of "a revolutionary army of the proletariat" that would "reconstruct the nation from the working class until class distinctions are eliminated."

Despite their natural antipathy, the Communists and Nationalists maintained a cautious coexistence for most of the 1920s. The CCP used this time to build its power base, especially among the lowly peasants whose plight was largely ignored by the GMD. In southern China, especially Jiangxi, Mao and his comrades experimented with mass mobilization and militarization of the peasantry, employing class-consciousness, land reform and the violent suppression of oppressive landlords. The strategy worked: CCP membership grew from about 1,000 members in 1925 to about 800,000 by 1940.

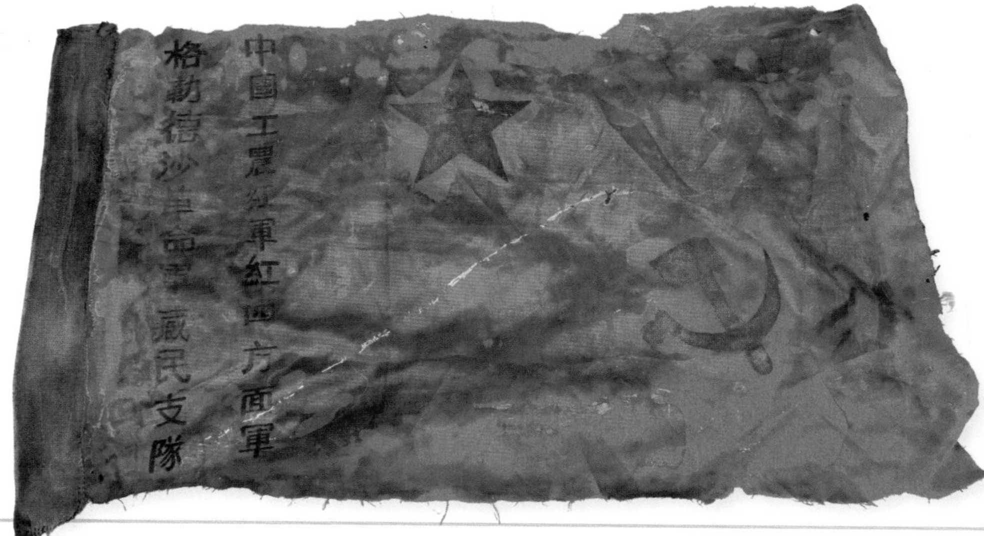

RIGHT This early Communist flag was left by the Red Army when it passed through the Danba area of Sichuan province in 1935. The words on the left identify it as belonging to the Tibetan Detachment of the Ge Le De Sha Revolutionary troops, Fourth Front Army.
LI FAN

ABOVE Young Mao played a role in the early days of both the Communist Party and Guomindang, when the parties enjoyed a measure of cooperation. In 1921, he attended the founding Congress of the CCP and three years later he was a delegate to the first National Conference of the GMD.
CHINA FOTOPRESS

Meanwhile, Moscow opened the Sun Yat-sen University of the Toilers of the East to train future party apparatchiks and civil servants. Both the CCP and GMD sent hundreds of Chinese to train there. Its graduates included Deng Xiaoping, future leader of the People's Republic of China.

In 1924 the Soviet Union also paid for the creation of the Whampoa Military Academy in Guangdong province. Chiang Kai-shek, a salt trader's son who became a Sun favorite in the GMD, was appointed its first commandant. Zhou Enlai, who had returned from studies in Europe, became a political instructor.

The GMD's power was based on a tacit alliance with moderate nationalists and merchants in the cities. The countryside, however, was still in the grip of warlords, exploitative landlords, bandit gangs and corrupt bureaucrats. The Communist Party chose to make the millions of oppressed peasants their main constituency. In a 1927 paper, Mao wrote that as the peasants' wrath grew, every Chinese had to choose from three alternatives: "March at their head and lead them. Trail behind them, gesticulating and criticizing. Or stand in their way and oppose them."

After Sun Yat-sen's death in 1925 and a period of instability and infighting, Chiang, widely known as the Generalissimo, took control of the GMD. Increasingly fearful of Communist progress in some provinces, he turned on the CCP in 1927. In Shanghai, Guangzhou and Changsha, the Nationalist leader ordered a massive purge. Thousands of Communists, and sometimes their wives and children, were slaughtered in what became known as the "April 12 Incident" or "the White Terror."

Future Chinese premier Zhou Enlai reportedly jumped through a window as would-be assassins arrived. He eventually ended up in Nanchang, where he organized an uprising against the GMD garrison. The uprising failed, but it marked the creation of the first formal units of the Red Army. In isolated redoubts, most of them in inaccessible areas of forests and mountains, the Communist army began to emerge.

By the beginning of the 1930s the seeds for the coming revolution had been planted, though initially the future looked far from promising.

In the Jinggang Mountains of Jiangxi province, Mao Zedong and a close comrade, Zhu De, formed the Jiangxi Soviet. Though Mao soon became Jiangxi's preeminent theoretician, many of his early colleagues looked down on him for his lack of formal university education or foreign travel. Hailing from from a remote part of Sichuan, Zhu was a former gym

"A revolution is not a dinner party, or writing an essay, or painting a picture, or doing embroidery; it cannot be so refined, so leisurely and gentle, so temperate, kind, courteous, restrained and magnanimous," Mao Zedong wrote in 1927. "A revolution is an insurrection, an act of violence by which one class overthrows another."

BELOW Although Chiang Kai-shek spent three months in the Soviet Union and later became the first commandant of the Soviet-funded Whampoa Military Academy, he soon became a staunch anti-Communist. As leader of the Guomindang, he ordered the violent suppression of CCP members in 1927.
CHINA FOTOPRESS

instructor turned minor warlord who had received some military training in Yunnan and Germany. After meeting Zhu in Germany, Zhou Enlai sponsored him for party membership.

The Jiangxi Soviet's military force was named the First Front Army. Beyond Jiangxi, other Red Army concentrations had formed, though the numbers they were given had little to do with their formation date, their location or, it sometimes seems, logic. The Second Front Army led by He Long, a former Nationalist general, was created in northern Hunan province, some 580 miles (950 kilometers) northwest of the First Front Army.

Zhang Guotao, a student leader at Beijing University who had attended the Communist Party's founding meeting in Shanghai, gathered a guerrilla force in Sichuan's mountainous north bordering Shaanxi province into what would become the Fourth Front Army. The Sixth Army Corps under 26-year-old Xiao Ke, the Red Army's youngest general, was based in the Jiangxi–Hunan border area, and the Seventh Front Army had gathered in Fujian province, southeast of Jiangxi.

Chiang mounted four so-called Encirclement Campaigns to eradicate these forces. All failed. But in Jiangxi in 1933, the Fifth Encirclement Campaign began to succeed …

CHAPTER 2

The Enemy Approaches

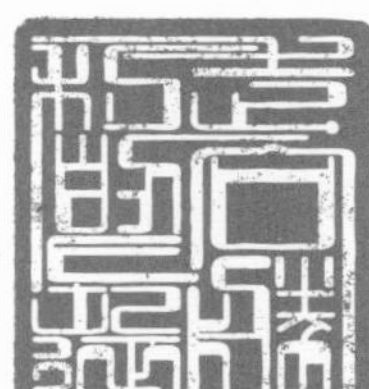

By mid-1933 the First Front Army was clustered around the village of Yeping, several miles from the Jiangxi Soviet's headquarters in Ruijin. The situation was grim. The soldiers were mostly illiterate, underfed peasants, and in recent fighting the revolutionaries had suffered some 60,000 casualties.

The First Front Army could muster about 180,000 men, including reserve formations, and perhaps 200,000 militia. They were poorly armed, with not enough rifles for everyone, no heavy artillery, little ammunition, few grenades or mortar shells, and three or four pilots for their handful of captured airplanes.

In the countryside beyond, the GMD had deployed about 900,000 troops, more than double the size of the Communist force. In 1933–34 alone, Generalissimo Chiang, backed by wealthy Chinese and foreign commercial interests, spent about US$20 million on state-of-the-art rifles, artillery and planes from the United States and Europe. From airfields across southern China, hundreds of Nationalist fighter-bombers patrolled the skies. Bombing raids and distant battlefield explosions became a constant reminder to the rebels of what could lie ahead.

LEFT In the late 1920s, Zhu De and Mao Zedong united their armies into a force that would form the core of the Red Army units that moved into the Ruijin area in 1929.
CHINA NATIONAL MUSEUM

LEFT Most of the women on the Long March were given supply and support work, though a few were allowed to fight as guerrillas. One young woman, Guo Chun-Qing, disguised herself as a man and received the Red Army's highest decoration after she was wounded in battle.
PEOPLE'S LIBERATION ARMY PHOTO ARCHIVE

The Red Army later became famous for its fortitude and stubborn courage, but in the early days these qualities were sometimes in short supply. "Whenever we passed through a village, some comrades would disappear into the houses and were never seen again," one Long Marcher later recalled.

Indeed, 28,000 troops deserted in November and December 1933, including 4,300 from Ruijin alone One document from a Jiangxi provincial archive reflects the CCP's growing alarm: "Three-quarters of the militia mobilized for the recent battles … ran away within the first few days, leaving barely a quarter … It is tantamount to helping the enemy. It cannot be tolerated."

To many in the Red Army, the Nationalists' juggernaut seemed all but unstoppable. Advised by General Alexander von Falkenhausen, a German veteran of World War I, the GMD had built an ever-tightening noose of forts around the Jiangxi Soviet. Red Army soldiers called these round brick blockhouses "turtle shells."

Each Nationalist battalion was ordered to build at least one blockhouse per week. By late 1934 there were 14,000 blockhouses linked by hundreds of miles of roads. The Red Army "will be finished this year," a GMD newspaper exulted.

From late 1933 until late 1934 the Jiangxi Soviet depended on advisors who were either Soviet-trained Chinese Bolsheviks or military officers sent by the Comintern. The most prominent foreign emissary was Otto Braun, a German-born agent who had trained in a Russian military academy. In China he used the *nom de guerre* Li De. A man with an overbearing manner, Li De was able to communicate directly with Moscow via radio, a fact that greatly enhanced his stature and power.

The Moscow faction believed that the Red Army should combat Chiang's advance with the sort of positional warfare that was widely used during World War I: occupy ground and prevent the enemy from taking it.

Mao Zedong had argued unsuccessfully that the Red Army should employ guerrilla tactics that focused more on speed and mobility. When Nationalist agents in Shanghai found and closed Li De's radio relay, cutting direct communications with Moscow, Mao saw his chance to press his view again. Perhaps a more Chinese approach might finally prevail?

Certainly, something had to be done. As Chiang's noose drew ever tighter

ABOVE The Red Army was constantly recruiting soldiers during the Long March, drawing on local peasants and members of minority ethnic groups. Although this group of fledgling soldiers hadn't learned to salute properly, and some didn't even have footwear, their enthusiasm and spirit are unmistakable.

PEOPLE'S LIBERATION ARMY PHOTO ARCHIVE

FOLLOWING PAGES Many of the Long March soldiers, such as these members of the Fourth Front Army, were barely out of their teens. Despite their youth, by the time they completed the 6,000-mile (10,000-kilometer) march, they were battle-hardened warriors.

YAN'AN REVOLUTIONARY MUSEUM

ABOVE Long March soldiers had to carry everything on their backs, despite the difficult terrain and sometimes harsh weather. While tubs such as these would have been heavy and awkward, they served many purposes: water carrier, washbasin, shelter from weather and a much-needed place to sit up off the ground.
PEOPLE'S LIBERATION ARMY PHOTO ARCHIVE

around the Jiangxi Soviet, the Red Army's leadership intensified their policy debate. A desperate decision was made: "We break out or we die!" A new territorial base had to be found, somewhere on the fringes of Nationalist power, where the Communists could regroup and organize with as little interference as possible.

Red Army troops received their first clue that a change of strategy was in the wind when they received a new issue of clothing. Jiangxi was enjoying warm late-summer temperatures in 1934, but Red Army quartermasters distributed cold-weather gear. Sandal makers were ordered to produce 200,000 pairs of grass sandals with thicker soles.

The new clothing would soon be needed. To the west and north of Jiangxi lay some of China's most inhospitable mountains and river valleys. Getting around at the time was extremely difficult. The Red Army faced narrow dirt or rubble roads, ramshackle bridges and uncharted river fords.

With winter closing in, no time remained for elaborate planning. To mislead Nationalist spies that the Jiangxi Soviet would stay and fight to the death, an impassioned message was circulated: "For the defense of our regime and of our lives, our children and babies, our land and grain, our cows, hogs, chickens and ducks, and for resistance against enemy slaughter, destruction, looting and rape, we should use our daggers, hunting guns, rifles and any sorts of old and new weapons to arm ourselves … We must win the final victory!"

But final victory remained a distant dream. On October 16, 1934, at eight points along the Yudu River near Ruijin, the Jiangxi Soviet launched that most extraordinary undertaking—a state on the move. In all, an estimated 86,000 soldiers and another 11,000 support personnel set off from the Jiangxi Soviet. What would come to be known as the Long March had begun.

There was no overall plan for the retreat and, anyway, military secrecy demanded that ordinary soldiers not be given detailed orders. Probably no one, not even Mao, knew that the army would eventually march the length of China.

One soldier would later recall young women, some of them the wives of departing troops, coming to the Yudu

ABOVE The Long Marchers passed through some of the world's most challenging and rugged terrain, including narrow paths on sheer cliff faces rising up from fast-flowing rivers. In addition to the ever-present danger of falling, these pathways left Red Army troops exposed to surprise attacks by Guomindang forces.

PEOPLE'S LIBERATION ARMY PHOTO ARCHIVE

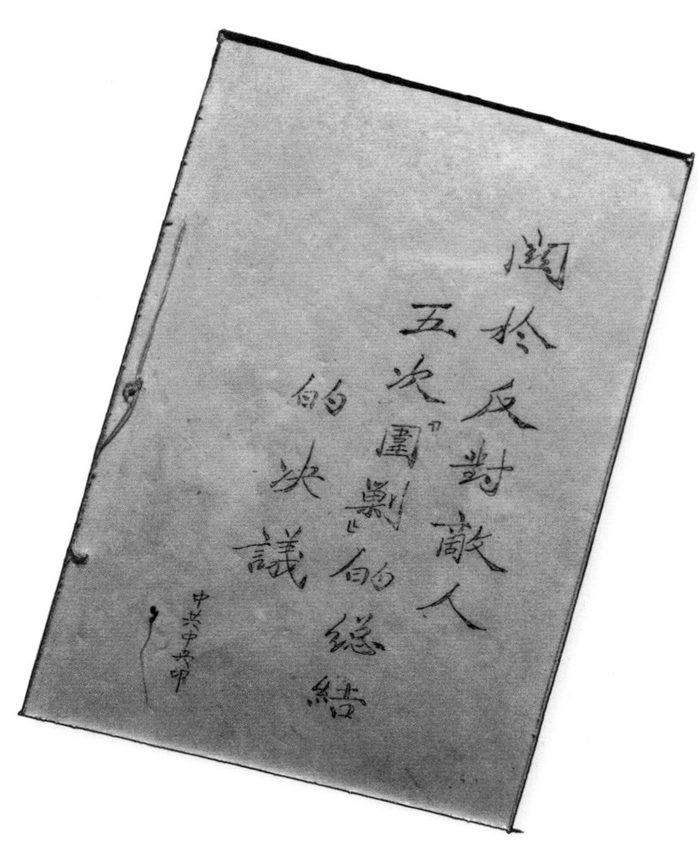

關於反對敵人
五次"圍剿"的總結
的決議
中共中央印

RIGHT This report, which documents the Red Army's resistance to the Fifth Encirclement Campaign, was passed by the Politburo of the Chinese Communist Party in February 1935 and distributed to members of the party's Central Committee.

CHINA NATIONAL MUSEUM

BELOW During the Long March, Red Army soldier Huang Zhen filled a logbook with sketches, providing some of the few images created during the march itself. Huang went on to become a well-known diplomat, serving as ambassador to Hungary, Indonesia and France, and later was appointed a Minister of Culture. This sketch shows Red Army troops crossing the Xiang River, site of an early and bloody battle with Nationalist forces.

HUANG ZHEN

RIGHT The bugle was the Red Army's single most important communication tool, both on the battlefield and during the daily troop movements of the Long March. The image of the bugle boy standing defiantly and sending out a call to arms, evokes the *esprit de corps* that was so vital to the success of the Long March.

YAN'AN REVOLUTIONARY MUSEUM

River to say good-bye. They sang an uplifting, though rather cheeky, song:

A model soldier,
That's what I want you to be.
I long for your good news
day and night,
My Red Army brother,
Capture a few generals
and make me happy!

The Long March was a "human undertaking [with] no parallel," Harrison Salisbury of *The New York Times* later wrote. "In it there is a little, perhaps, of the exodus of the Jews, a little of Hannibal's crossing of the Alps, of Napoleon's march on Moscow, and, to my surprise, some echoes of America's winning of the West, the great cavalcade over mountain and prairie.

"But no comparison fits. The Long March is *sui generis.* Its heroism has fired the dreams of a nation ... and set China moving toward a destiny no man can yet divine."

At first, the Red Army's exodus went undetected. The 28,000-man main force, with Zhu De as commander-in-chief and Zhou Enlai as political commissar, moved in three columns to the west and south. Another 66,000 men defended the flanks and carried rice and salt rations. Zhou's troops carried only 9,000 rifles, each with a pitiful hundred or so cartridges. Machine guns, numbering just 300, were limited to 10 minutes of automatic fire per weapon.

Up and down all but impenetrable terrain, soldiers and thousands of porters shouldering poles carried food and medical supplies, generators, printing presses and miscellaneous camp equipment—a cavalcade of soldiers, porters, horses, donkeys and mules that stretched for 50 miles (80 kilometers).

Considering that the army was in retreat and faced enormous hazards, morale was surprisingly high. Encouraged by their officers and political cadres, the troops sang marching songs and shouted party slogans:

Comrades! Ready with your guns!
Charge with one heart,
Struggle and fight to kill!
Comrades! Fight for freedom!
Fight for the Soviets!

The Nationalists realized that the battlefield was changing when the vanguard of the retreating forces fell upon the first "turtle shell" fortifications. The Red Army's early advance came swiftly: the line in Jiangxi was broken on October 21; Hunan on November 3 and again on November 10. But the toll on the revolutionary forces was high: in one continuous five-day engagement 4,000 Communist soldiers were killed.

Crossing the Xiang River in late November and early December was the first great battle of the Long March. First Front Army political commissar Nie Rongzhen remembered it as "the Long March's most dangerous days."

The revolutionaries had known what was in store: Nationalist warplanes were dropping leaflets designed to demoralize them: "Communist bandits! The high command ordered that we wait for you … Hurry up! We beg you. We beg you. We have fixed up a dandy little trap for you."

GMD troops poured down on the revolutionaries' river-crossing points. The river was fordable, but the enemies' blockhouses and troop concentrations formed a terrifying barrier. "The river was like a bath full of blood," a Xiang River battle survivor later recalled. "There were so many bodies floating on the water, like dead locusts … I held on to a floating body [and] paddled … It took me ages to cross."

The First Front Army crossed this major barrier, but victory came at a very high price. By some counts as many as 30,000 men were killed or injured, or simply deserted the Red Army, between November 25 and December 3.

At around this time soldiers of the 6th Army Corps in Zhenyuan, some 300 miles (500 kilometers) northwest of the First Front Army, captured a group of Protestant missionaries. One of them, Rudolf Bosshardt, later wrote a memoir, *The Restraining Hand*, that offered some unique insights into the Long March.

Bosshardt described a time when Chinese revolutionaries were still inspired by the young Soviet Union. Whenever the Red Army halted for any length of time, a room was selected to be a "Lenin Hall" and decorated with evergreens, paper flowers, flags and pictures of Marx and Lenin.

The missionary witnessed Red Army interviews of new recruits. When officers asked why they wanted to join the Red Army, Bosshardt wrote, "Invariably they answered: 'Because we do not have enough to eat at home.'"

He also described the execution of cruel landlords, as well as the trial and execution of a man who had attempted, in exchange for a bribe, to hide a landlord from the Red Army.

Meanwhile, a spirited rearguard of 6,000 troops harassed GMD efforts to occupy the abandoned Red Army bases in Jiangxi and Fujian, putting into action the guerrilla tactics championed by Mao and Zhu De. One version of

LEFT One of the keys to the Red Army's success during the Long March was its ability to constantly replenish troop numbers. As it moved across China, the army engaged with the local population, recruiting disenfranchised farmers and peasants and training them in guerrilla warfare and militia duties. "The Red Army are the fish and the people are the ocean," Mao once said.

PEOPLE'S LIBERATION ARMY PHOTO ARCHIVE

"In the last few days' march we did badly with our discipline," wrote future paramount leader Deng Xiaoping in Red Star, *the Long March newspaper he edited, on November 11, 1934. "People do not listen to our sweet talk; they observe our actions. An army without discipline will not win their sympathy and support, no matter how much propaganda we do."*

the guerrilla credo was rendered in 16 Chinese characters:

> *The enemy approaches, we retreat.*
> *The enemy halts, we move in.*
> *The enemy tires, we attack.*
> *The enemy retreats, we pursue.*

The shortage of ammunition contributed to the revolutionaries' ferocity in battle. The Red Army encouraged a battle cry: "Three bullets for a charge!" They specialized in close-combat fighting, slashing at the enemy with sword and bayonet as they shouted "*Sha! Sha! Sha!*" ("Kill! Kill! Kill!"). The thought of what would happen if they lost also motivated the rebels: Chiang's army routinely massacred fallen and captured enemy soldiers.

In the wake of the terrible losses at Xiang River, the possibility of failure was looming larger. The Red Army had lost some two-thirds of its original force, and word came that warlord troops from Hunan were closing in from the east.

At the same time, another battle gripped the Long March: the struggle for power within the leadership group. The original plan was to head north from Jiangxi to Hunan, where the First Front Army would join up with Communist forces in the area. The Moscow-aligned faction wanted to stay the course. The army commanders refused, on the grounds that they would be wiped out by an overwhelming force of GMD and warlord troops.

With his influence on the rise, Mao argued that the Red Army should avoid positional warfare, develop more mobile tactics and, instead of continuing north, move northwest to set up a new base near the border of Guizhou and Sichuan.

ABOVE This meeting hall in Hunan remains largely as it was when the Second Front Army and the Fourth Front Army came together there in November 1934. The images of Marx and Lenin on the wall reflect the influence that advisors from the Soviet Union's Comintern held over the Red Army in the early days of the Long March.

FENG JIANGUO

CHAPTER 3

Mao in Command

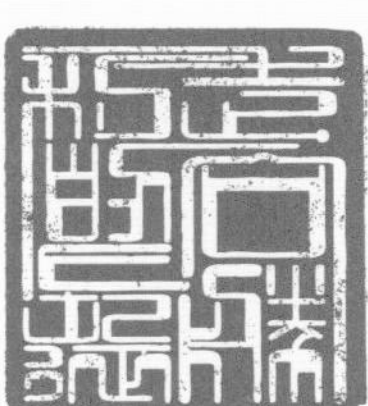

Discussions continued until the leaders reached Zunyi. Outside its walls the Red Army fought pitched battles with troops of the warlord Bai Huizhang. When Zunyi, a town of perhaps 50,000, had fallen, the Red Army paraded in, singing "The Three Main Rules of Discipline and the Eight Points for Attention":

THE RULES:
Obey orders in all your actions.
Don't take a needle or a piece of thread
from the people.
Turn in everything you capture.

THE POINTS OF ATTENTION:
Speak politely.
Pay fairly for what you buy.
Return everything you borrow.
Pay for any damage.
Don't strike or swear at people.
Don't damage the crops.
Don't take liberties with women.
Don't mistreat captives.

LEFT This hand-colored photograph is one of the best known images of the young Mao. It was taken in Yan'an in July 1936 when he met Edgar Snow, the first Western journalist to interview the Communist leader. Mao's "clothes were neat but his hair was somewhat ruffled," an eyewitness recounted. "So Snow took off his own brand new army cap with the red star and suggested the Chairman wear it."
YAN'AN REVOLUTIONARY MUSEUM

BELOW When the Red Army captured the Loushan Pass and returned to Zunyi in late February 1935, they took 3,000 enemy soldiers prisoner. This sketch by Huang Zhen shows captive officers and soldiers gathered for a meal. "The captives, formerly laboring people who served the Guomindang army under force, were deeply affected by our rules for treating prisoners of war," Huang wrote. "After a short period of education, most of the captives volunteered to join the Red Army."

HUANG ZHEN

RIGHT News of the Zunyi Conference and Mao Zedong's rise to power spread quickly. This is the original communiqué written by Chen Yun in Russian for the Comintern officials describing the Long March and the results of the Zunyi Conference in January 1935. Chen Yun would go on to be an influential Communist Party leader, serving as a Politburo Standing Committee member from 1977 to 1987.

CHINA NATIONAL MUSEUM

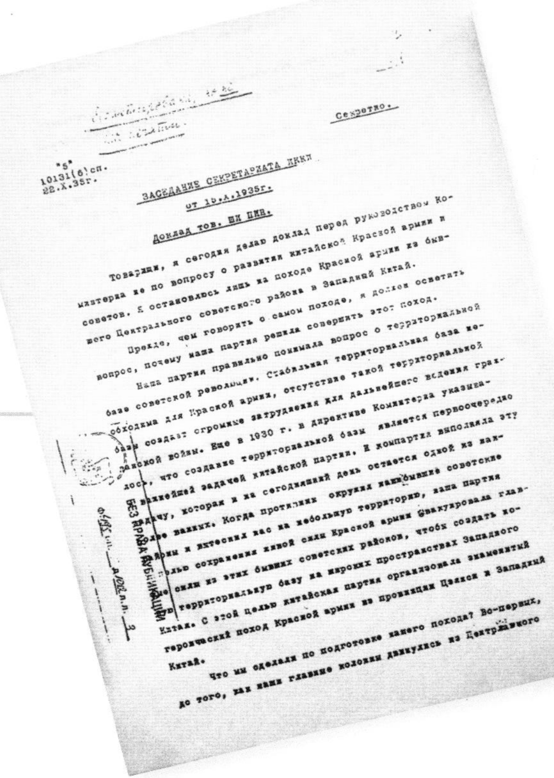

"5"
10131(6)сп.
22.X.35г.

Секретно.

ЗАСЕДАНИЕ СЕКРЕТАРИАТА ИККИ

от 15.X.1935г.

Доклад тов. ШИ ПИН.

Товарищи, я сегодня делаю доклад перед руководством Коминтерна не по вопросу о развитии китайской Красной армии и советов. Я остановлюсь лишь на походе Красной армии из бывшего Центрального советского района в Западный Китай.

Прежде, чем говорить о самом походе, я должен осветить вопрос, почему наша партия решила совершить этот поход.

Наша партия правильно понимала вопрос о территориальной базе советской революции. Стабильная территориальная база необходима для Красной армии, отсутствие такой территориальной базы создает огромные затруднения для дальнейшего ведения гражданской войны. Еще в 1930 г. в директиве Коминтерна указывалось, что создание территориальной базы является первоочередной важнейшей задачей китайской партии. И компартия выполняла эту задачу, которая и на сегодняшний день остается одной из важнейших. Когда противник окружил наши бывшие советские районы и вытеснил нас на небольшую территорию, наша партия с целью сохранения живой силы Красной армии эвакуировала главные силы из этих бывших советских районов, чтобы создать новую территориальную базу на широких пространствах Западного Китая. С этой целью китайская партия организовала знаменитый героический поход Красной армии из провинции Цзянси в Западный Китай.

Что мы сделали по подготовке нашего похода? Во-первых, до того, как наши главные колонны двинулись из Центрального

БЕЗ ПРАВА ПУБЛИКАЦИИ

The CCP Politburo scheduled a conference for Zunyi. Mao swung into action, enlisting supporters and writing a detailed review of his policy proposals. Twenty of the highest-ranking comrades gathered on January 15, 1935, in a building from which Bai Huizhang had been chased. In a sometimes-heated hour-long address, Mao blamed the Moscow faction, and especially Li De, for most of the battlefield disasters.

Later the conference passed a resolution accusing the Comintern's emissary of incompetence, of using punishment rather than reason to suppress disagreement and of practicing "adventurism in attack."

It is difficult to exaggerate the Zunyi Conference's importance to the history of modern China. After three days of meetings, Mao regained his position in

the Politburo's all-powerful Standing Committee and, most significantly, became the dominant theorist of the unfolding revolution.

Zhou Enlai, who had earlier resisted many of Mao's ideas, now supported him. Their alliance—Mao as paramount leader and Zhou as loyal aide—would last more than four decades.

Zhou and Zhu De were placed in command of military operations, but everyone understood that the Red Army would be implementing Mao's directives on strategy and political direction. Instructions from the Comintern were no longer followed.

For the moment, there was much to be done. When the Red Army moved out of Zunyi on January 19, an estimated 36,000 troops remained of the 86,000 or so who had left Jiangxi. A vast wilderness of mountains, jungle and swampy grasslands lay ahead.

To make matters worse, Chiang had mustered about 400,000 troops near Chongqing just to the First Front Army's north. Mao had had to abandon a plan to join forces under He Long and Xiao Ke in Hunan–Hubei–Guizhou. Instead, they would try to find the Fourth Front Army under Zhang Guotao. Thanks to primitive, and usually non-existent, communications, Mao had no clear knowledge of Zhang's fortunes or plans.

But some factors played out in Mao's favor. The Xiang River battle had forced the Red Army to reduce the size of its baggage train. Office equipment or anything not directly associated with combat was abandoned. A core of battle-hardened troops capable of marching 40 miles (65 kilometers) a day was steeled for the coming ordeal. Here was the revolutionary force of mobility and grit that Mao had long championed.

The march out of Zunyi offered one of the more dramatic images of the Long March. The road was, for once, something more than a dirt track. Mao rode on a big white horse, Zhu De at his side. The pair had become so inseparable that people began to speak of a single great revolutionary called Zhu–Mao.

In addition to settling crucial questions of leadership and strategy, the Zunyi Conference had presented the Red Army with a supplementary purpose. In 1931 Japan had launched a full-scale invasion of Manchuria and was clearly preparing an attack on China proper. The revolutionaries now had

TOP LEFT Following the Zunyi Conference, Mao's position as undisputed leader of the Communist Party was secure.
PEOPLE'S LIBERATION ARMY PHOTO ARCHIVE

TOP CENTER Zhu De was named Military Chairman of the Central Revolutionary Military Committee, putting him in charge of the Red Army for the Long March.
PEOPLE'S LIBERATION ARMY PHOTO ARCHIVE

TOP RIGHT In the months after the Zunyi Conference, Zhou Enlai effectively became second-in-command of the Chinese Communist Party, a position he held until his death in 1976.
PEOPLE'S LIBERATION ARMY PHOTO ARCHIVE

LEFT Mao Zedong rose from humble beginnings as the son of a Hunanese farmer to become the architect and founding father of the People's Republic of China. When asked at the completion of the Long March about its significance, Mao called it a "seeding machine. In the eleven provinces it has sown many seeds which will sprout, leaf, blossom and bear fruit, and will yield a harvest in the future."
YAN'AN REVOLUTIONARY MUSEUM

two powerful enemies—Chiang and the Japanese emperor.

Red Army soldiers began painting a slogan on the walls of towns through which they marched: "Resist Japan; Oppose Chiang." The need for the First Front Army to join forces with Zhang Guotao in northern Sichuan had become even more pressing.

To get there the First Front Army had to cross central China's greatest barrier, the Yangzi River. And at the key river port of Chongqing, and in Guizhou province, Chiang was once again gathering forces for a final strike.

Four times in as many weeks in early 1935 the Red Army crossed the Chishui River, a tributary of the Yangzi. A battle at Qinggangpo, which Mao had thought would be an easy encounter with the army of a notoriously ineffectual Guizhou warlord, took an unexpected turn when some of Chiang's best forces entered the fighting.

For a time the Red Army faced the possibility of defeat. At one point Zhu De's wife narrowly escaped an ambush. Then a crack regiment—the high command's guards brigade—was called in to hold off the enemy while the Red Army organized a prudent withdrawal.

Crossing the Yangzi River and moving into Sichuan was postponed for the

moment. Instead, the Red Army moved toward Yunnan.

The Long March had many tragedies, and even the mightiest leaders were not spared personal suffering. Before the Long March began Mao's young wife, He Zizhen, had become pregnant. In February 1935, at a place thought to have been near the Yunnan border, she gave birth to a daughter. With GMD warplanes harassing the moving columns, the couple could not keep the infant girl. He was forced to turn the unnamed baby over to a peasant couple. The daughter's fate remains a mystery to this day.

In winter Yunnan can be a cold, grim place. Mao and his troops reached Zhaxi in northern Yunnan early in February, as the Year of the Dog became the Year of the Pig. But there was little food for New Year feasts and few reasons for celebration. An icy rain fell, turning to snow in the night. Word came that Chiang was again positioning his troops to crush the Red Army as it attempted another crossing of the Yangzi.

But Chiang had become predictable on the battlefield. The Red Army's marching and counter-marching repeatedly confused the GMD troops. This time Mao had the First Front

ABOVE The battle of Qinggangpo on January 28, 1935, proved to be Mao's first test as leader. Both the Communists and the Nationalists suffered thousands of casualties before the Red Army decided to retreat. The battle is remarkable for the large number of future Red Army and Communist Party leaders who joined the fighting: three state presidents, one premier, five ministers of defense, eight supreme commanders and 150 generals.
CATHERINE CROLL

If we save the mountain, we'll have wood.
If we save the river, we'll have fish to fry.
If we save the Revolution, we'll have our own land.
If we save the Soviet, red flags will fly.

Song by folk singer Wang Quanyuan (a.k.a. "Golden Throat")

LEFT The Red Army used slogans and messages to great effect as they moved through towns and villages during the Long March. This message, reproduced at the Chishui Memorial Hall museum, declares: "If you do not want to be starving and get beaten by the White Army [the Red Army's name for the Guomindang forces], then join the Red Army!"
CATHERINE CROLL

Army double back on its tracks, reenter Guizhou province, take the strategic Loushan Pass and once again occupy Zunyi.

An exultant Mao celebrated the Loushan Pass victory with his first poem of the Long March:

> *Idle boast the strong pass*
> *is a wall of iron,*
> *We are crossing its summit,*
> *The rolling hills sea-blue,*
> *The dying sun blood-red.*

As they returned to Zunyi, Chiang's forces moved into position at river crossings in western Guizhou. In hand-to-hand fighting the Red Army routed two GMD divisions, its first major triumph of the Long March and a major boost to troop morale.

But it was April 1935 and the First Front Army was still in Guizhou; the Yangzi had yet to be crossed. Mao once again compensated for his lack of strength by resorting to subterfuge. The Communists pretended to assault Guiyang. When Chiang brought in troops from further west to repel the attack, the Red Army switched direction, driving through the newly opened gap in the GMD's defenses.

After further maneuvers that confused the Nationalists, the Red Army moved even further west.

As the First Front Army positioned itself yet again to cross the Yangzi River, the revolutionaries faced difficulties elsewhere. The Fourth Front Army had retreated to the Xikang plateaus in remote northwest Sichuan province. Now hundreds of miles separated the two armies, too far for the Fourth Front troops to support their comrades during the river crossing.

But any further delay in crossing the Yangzi could give the Nationalists time to tighten their encirclement. So the Communists headed west once more, again moving in a back-and-forth pattern to keep the enemy guessing. Chiang, flying from Chongqing to Guiyang, read these apparently erratic movements as the death throes of a bewildered, defeated army. Convinced that they were heading for his headquarters in Guiyang, he prepared his guard troops for a hurried evacuation. Then word came of artillery fire near Yunnanfu, Yunnan's capital, today known as Kunming.

It was another deception devised by Mao. As GMD divisions headed for

BELOW At Loushan Pass the Red Army routed two Guomindang divisions, marking its first major victory since the start of the Long March. "We cut them down with broadswords and hand grenades," a Red Army political officer said. "The main body fled south. Most of them were wiped out."
PEOPLE'S LIBERATION ARMY PHOTO ARCHIVE

Yunnanfu, the mass of the First Front Army made for the upper reaches of the Yangzi, where the river bears the name Golden Sands. This country of deep ravines had no bridges and few ferries at the time. Chiang was convinced that crossing there was impossible, but the Red Army troops again demonstrated their skill in battlefield deception.

One battalion covered 85 miles (135 kilometers) in a day and a night, jogging much of the way to an upriver beachhead at Jiaopingdu, taking the defenders by surprise. With all the ferryboats on the far side of the river, a captured official was forced to order the guards to send over a ferry, allegedly for a GMD force that had unexpectedly arrived. The boat returned packed with revolutionaries who captured the surprised defenders in the middle of a mahjongg game.

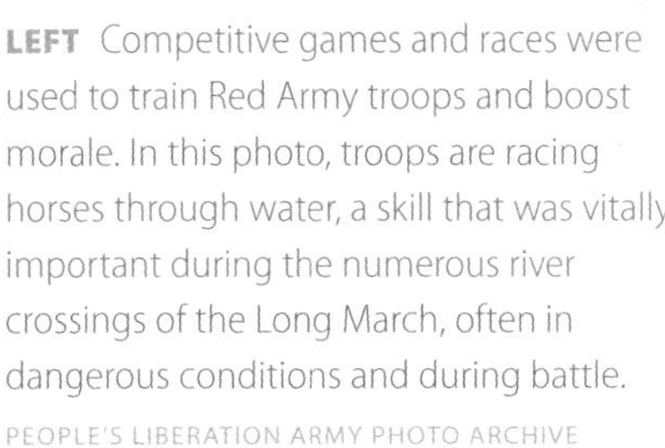

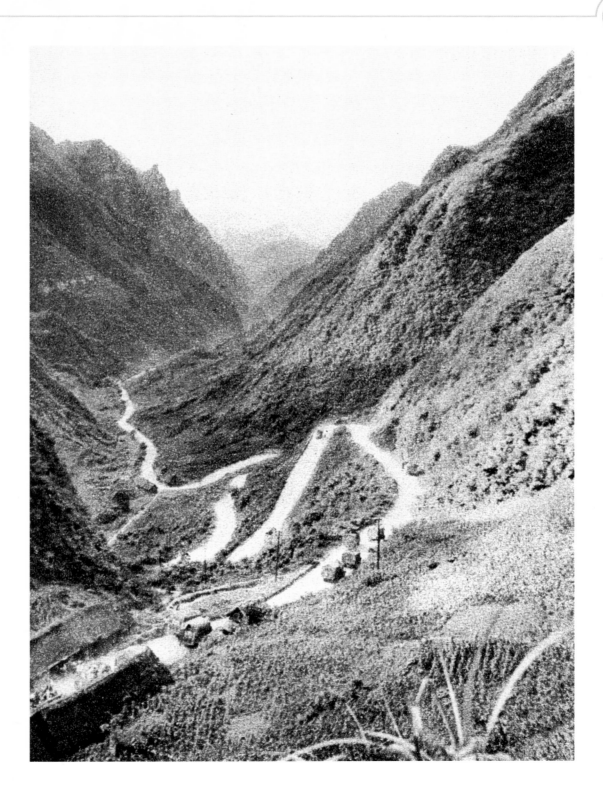

LEFT Competitive games and races were used to train Red Army troops and boost morale. In this photo, troops are racing horses through water, a skill that was vitally important during the numerous river crossings of the Long March, often in dangerous conditions and during battle.
PEOPLE'S LIBERATION ARMY PHOTO ARCHIVE

"The decisive battles in the coming months will decide whether we live or die … this is total war," declared the Central Committee of the Chinese Communist Party in May 1934 in a call for more soldiers. "Every member of the toiling masses should prepare to shed his last drop of blood at the front!"

PREVIOUS PAGES This photo was taken as the 6th Army Corps of the Red Army passed through Guizhou during the Long March. Wang Zhen, standing on the far left, is shown meeting with members of the Miao ethnic minority group. Wang would later become vice president of the People's Republic.
ZUNYI CONFERENCE MEMORIAL MUSEUM

BELOW "Oppressed and exploited by the Guomindang warlords and local landlords, the poverty-stricken salt carriers in Guizhou and Sichuan lived worse than beasts of burden," wrote Huang Zhen. "They were in such extreme poverty that people in other regions could not imagine it." Huang said the salt carriers warmly welcomed the Red Army, and many joined the Long March.
HUANG ZHEN

By noon of the following day—May 7, 1935—the Red Army's main forces had arrived at Jiaopingdu, and they quickly crossed the river in six large boats. When pursuing GMD troops reached the area four days later, the Communist rearguard taunted them from the far shore. "Come over. The water's fine!" they shouted. Those foolish enough to try were gunned down as they swam.

The First Front Army had shaken off its pursuers, but Chiang Kai-shek still hoped to seal his enemy's escape route at another strategically important river, the famed Dadu. The heroes of the ancient romance, *The Three Kingdoms*, had met their deaths on its banks some 1700 years earlier; and only a hundred years before the Red Army's arrival, the last survivors of the Taiping Rebellion had been wiped out by the Manchu emperor's troops at the same spot.

Chiang urged his generals and warlord allies to repeat the victory over the Taipings by wiping out the Communists as they tried to cross the Dadu River. But the revolutionaries also knew their history: the Taipings had paused for three days when they reached the river, giving the emperor's troops time to cut off their line of retreat. Mao was determined not to repeat the error.

By now the forced marching was taking its toll on the troops. Despite resistance to continued marching

within the ranks, a quick Politburo meeting outside the town of Huili ordered a relentless advance.

Concerns were no doubt heightened by the fact that they were passing through the territories of the Yi, a fierce Sino-Burmese minority group renowned for their dislike of strangers. The Red Army's policy of treating minority groups well, in contrast to the harsh approach taken by warlords and business interests, helped smooth relations with the Yi.

The Red Army began by releasing a number of Yi chieftains who had been imprisoned by the provincial government. They were taken with advancing First Front units and encouraged to speak on the revolutionaries' behalf to distrustful tribespeople. Liu Bocheng, a Red Army commander known as "One-Eyed Dragon" who spoke the local language, joined the Yi chief in drinking a toast in cockerel's blood, a solemn ritual of eternal brotherhood. To seal the alliance the Red Army presented weapons and ammunition to the Yi warriors.

The tribesmen reciprocated by leading the revolutionaries along mountain trails deep in the forest, concealing their movements from GMD reconnaissance planes. By late May 1935 they had reached the heights above Anshunchang, a hamlet on the Dadu River. What happened next is perhaps the Long March's most famous episode.

ABOVE Red Army commander Liu Bocheng helped end hostilities with the combative Yi people by drinking cockerel's blood with Yi tribesman Xiao Yedan. It proved to be a significant boost for Red Army soldiers as they approached the Dadu River.

WUQI LONG MARCH VICTORY MUSEUM

CHAPTER 4

The Bridge of Iron Chains

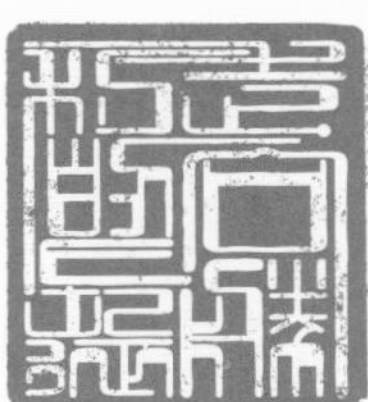

The forested chasms along the Dadu River have a long and brutal history. Both the Tea Route, used to carry China's most famous drink via Yunnan to Burma and India, and one branch of the Silk Road ran through the area. Generations of untamed tribes lived on the plunder taken from hapless traders.

This area was also the scene of one of the worst tragedies in Chinese history. In 1786 an earthquake caused a landslide that interrupted the Dadu River's flow. For ten days water backed up, eventually causing the dam to break. Towns and villages up to 860 miles (1,400 kilometers) downstream were flooded and more than 100,000 people died, still one of the deadliest landslide disasters in history.

As the vanguard of the First Front Army pushed across west Sichuan's wildest territory, cadres braced marchers for the coming engagement.

LEFT Seizing control of the Luding Bridge over the Dadu River was a do-or-die moment for the Red Army. The battle, one of the most celebrated engagements of the Long March, has been immortalized in hundreds of paintings.

WUQI LONG MARCH VICTORY MUSEUM

BELOW The Guomindang forces at the Dadu River tried to slow down the Red Army by pulling planks off the Luding Bridge, exposing the iron chains below. While troops went in search of wood to rebuild the bridge, a small contingent crawled along the chains, then charged the Nationalist troops at the far end of the bridge.

YAN'AN REVOLUTIONARY MUSEUM

RIGHT During his visit to the Red Army in 1936, American journalist and author Edgar Snow (third from the left) met some of the soldiers who fought in the battle for the Luding Bridge.

YAN'AN REVOLUTIONARY MUSEUM

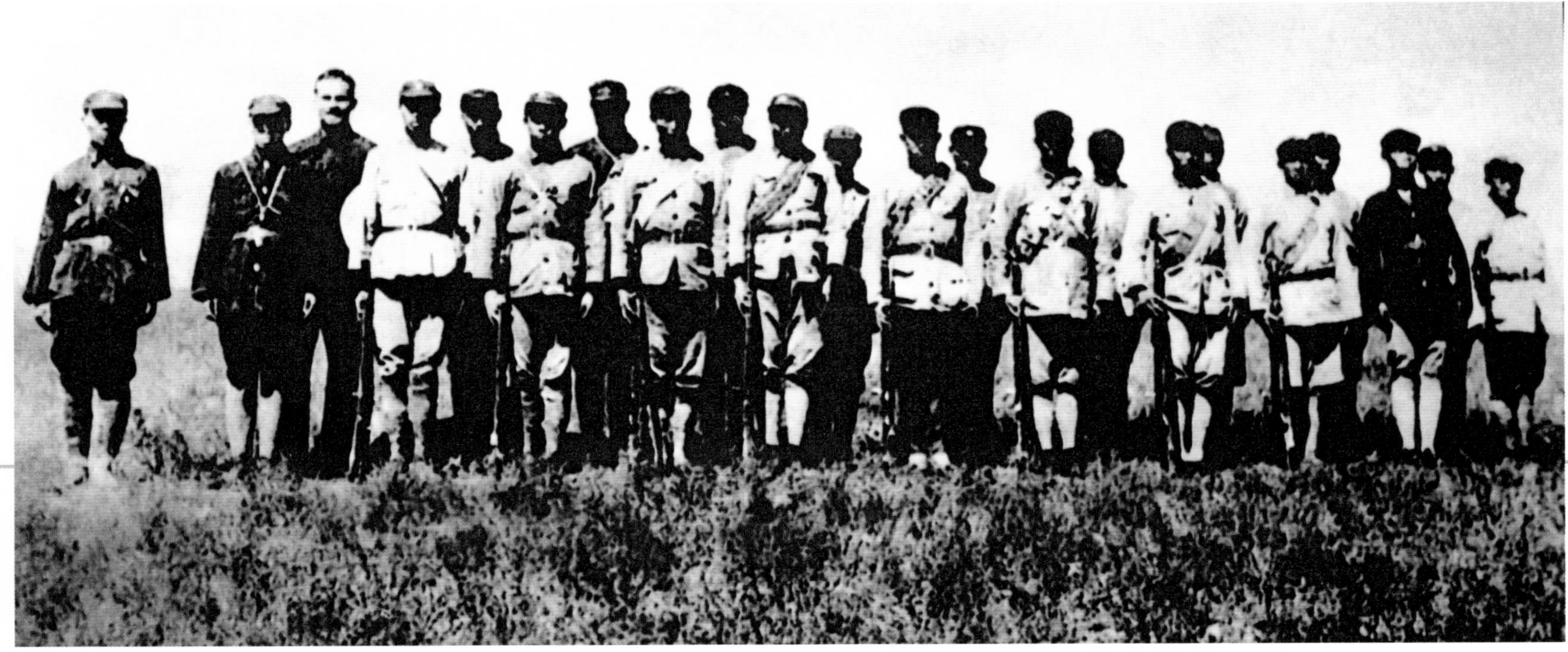

The Dadu River operation began with a couple of lucky breaks. The Nationalists had left a ferryboat on the Red Army's side of the river. Then Communist soldiers stumbled upon—and quickly captured—the local GMD commander, who was visiting friends and relatives in Anshunchang. Using his boat, Red Army troops were able to move along the river and capture two other ferries. For three days and nights a full division ferried itself across the river.

But more Red Army troops began appearing on the riverbanks—far too many for the three boats to move quickly. GMD planes bombed and strafed the concentrations and dropped leaflets that gleefully predicted the Red Army's annihilation. The pursuing Nationalists once again maneuvered into place for the kill.

The Red Army faced three options: cross the river, surrender or die. Mao and his closest leaders turned their attention to Luding Bridge, a 230-year-old river crossing built by Qing dynasty engineers.

Thirteen iron chains support wooden planks swinging above a raging, snow-fed mountain torrent. An early 20th-century Western visitor called it "a tenuous cobweb of man's ingenuity." The bridge was not designed to handle

RIGHT For three days, Red Army soldiers crossed the Dadu River at Anshunchang, using boats either left by or captured from the Nationalists. Huang Zhen described the treacherous waters: "With 300 meters [1,000 feet] in width and more than a dozen meters [40 feet] in depth, the river had a swift current of four meters [12 feet] a second, high waves and numerous whirlpools."
HUANG ZHEN

BELOW As it moved into new areas, the Red Army worked hard to build good relations with local villagers and tribesmen, an approach that won over ethnic minorities who had suffered at the hands of the Guomindang and local warlords. This sketch by Huang Zhen shows a Yi guide wearing a long cloak known as a caerwa and carrying a gun supplied by the Red Army. Despite the often rugged terrain, he was barefoot.

HUANG ZHEN

large numbers of people, but now the Red Army had little choice.

The vanguard, which had crossed in the ferries to Anshunchang, marched along the eastern bank, where they would attack the Nationalist troops guarding the bridge from the rear. The main force moved along the western shore and would stage a frontal assault.

On the second day, the vanguard met enemy resistance and fell behind. When the main column reached the Luding Bridge at dawn on May 30, Nationalist troops launched a mortar attack and began stripping wooden planks from the bridge.

For the moment the revolutionaries could not cross the bridge. All the planking had been torn up for more than 260 feet (80 meters) from the river's western bank. The iron chains swayed loosely over the rushing river. To replace the missing planks, Red Army soldiers hurriedly felled trees and wrenched doors from nearby houses.

Meanwhile, 22 soldiers volunteered to launch the primary assault. Captain Liao Dazhu, company commander, ran to the bridge, straddled one of the chains and worked his way toward the eastern bank, followed by his men armed with Tommy guns, pistols and grenades. Automatic weapons fire from the

ABOVE The Red Army's survival depended on crossing the many wild rivers of the west and northwest. The prospect of marching across rickety, swaying bridges must have struck terror in the soldiers' hearts.

PEOPLE'S LIBERATION ARMY PHOTO ARCHIVE

Down with the landlords who eat our flesh!
Down with the militarists who drink our blood!
Down with the traitors who sell China to Japan!
Welcome to the United Front with all anti-Japanese armies!
Long live the Chinese Revolution!
Long live the Chinese Red Army!

Poster quoted by Edgar Snow

"Our difficulties are great and our enemies many, but there is no mountain and no river we cannot cross, no fort we cannot conquer," Red Army commander Zhu De declared after the victory at the Luding Bridge.

BELOW While trekking along the rivers of central Sichuan, the Red Army had to negotiate narrow, winding tracks that sat above fast-moving waters and left them exposed to attack by Guomindang troops and airplanes.
YAN'AN REVOLUTIONARY MUSEUM

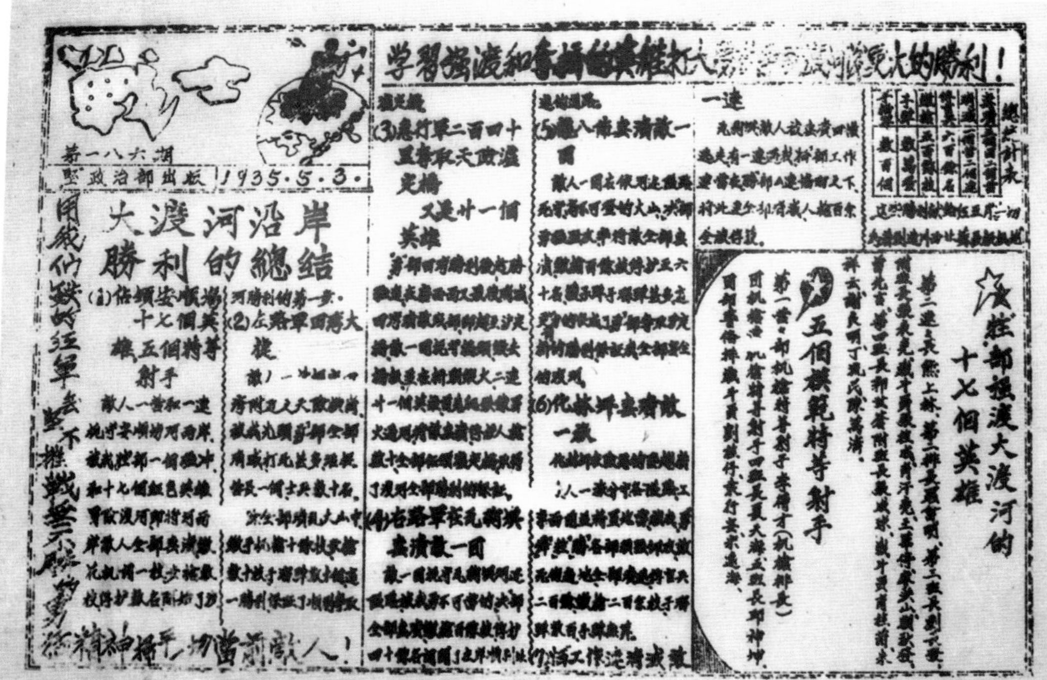

第一八六期

政治部出版 1935.5.3.

大渡河沿岸
勝利的總结

十七個英雄

五個模範特等射手

RIGHT This issue of *The Soldier* newspaper, which was distributed to revolutionary bases throughout China, reported on the Red Army's successful crossing of the Dadu River. The Red Army's ability to gather and distribute information was crucial to their success in winning the hearts and minds of both their own soldiers and ordinary Chinese.

WUQI LONG MARCH VICTORY MUSEUM

Nationalist troops raked along the chains.

The young company commander was hit and fell to his death. Four more revolutionaries were killed but the rest pushed ahead, chain link by chain link, and then across planks on which the Nationalists had poured burning kerosene.

An officer managed to clamber on to the flooring while avoiding the flames and yelled at the others to follow. Onlookers saw them disappear into the smoke, hurling hand grenades. Soon the GMD defenders turned and fled.

Cheering broke out as the improvised wooden planks thudded into position and a mass of men began moving across the bridge. GMD bombers pressed their attack but the battle was over. According to the official Red Army history of the battle, 17 men were lost in the taking of the Luding Bridge.

"Our difficulties are great and our enemies many, but there is no mountain and no river we cannot cross, no fort we cannot conquer," Zhu De declared at a memorial meeting that night to honor lost heroes. Yet the events leading up to the Dadu River battle told a grim story: only an estimated 13,000 rebels were left to cross the bridge.

Three days after the battle, Mao reached the bridge, walked across rickety planks that swayed above the river like a hammock and sat down with his high command for a celebratory banquet.

But the discussion could not have been altogether joyous: some of China's worst natural hazards—the Great Snow Mountains and treacherous swamplands—lay ahead. And the First Front Army still faced a disconcerting question: where were their Fourth Front Army comrades?

BELOW Grass sandals, the main form of footwear for Communist troops, are one of the enduring symbols of the Long March. Before the start of the Long March the Soviet Womens Department of the Red Army was reportedly ordered to produce grass shoes for the retreat.

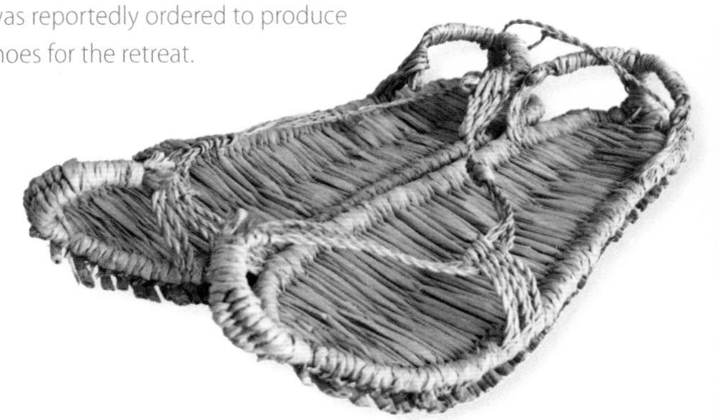

CHAPTER 5

Miracle in the Mountains

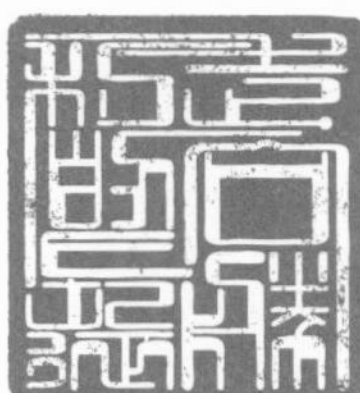

Mao appears to have guessed that Zhang Guotao's Fourth Front Army was somewhere beyond Hadapu. This medicine-distribution center lay to the north of Jiajin, a perpetually snow-covered peak known as the Faery Mountain because, as locals told the Red Army, it was too high for birds to fly over. Only angels could cross it.

The First Front Army paused for several days while medical orderlies instructed soldiers how to survive the snow, cold and high altitude of Jiajin. Strips of cloth over the eyes would provide a rough guard against snow blindness. As usual, the instructions were turned into a marching song:

The Jiajin Mountain is very high—
We must pay attention.
Wrap your feet and rub them well.
Don't take any rest at the top.
You must climb the mountain.
If the sick can't walk
We must help them.

LEFT After the daring victory at the Dadu River, the trek across the Great Snow Mountains must have felt like a slap in the face. Thousands of men died in the brutal conditions, but the First Front Army pressed on, desperate to find the Fourth Front Army.
CHINA NATIONAL MUSEUM

RIGHT Horses were mainly used as pack animals during the Long March, though the steep mountain crossings took their toll. "Many horses fell and broke their legs; only the mules kept their footing," Li De wrote in his memoirs. "There was hardly anything to eat in the mountains. Soldiers sliced flesh from dead horses until nothing but the skeleton remained."

PEOPLE'S LIBERATION ARMY PHOTO ARCHIVE

LEFT "The weather was changeable in the snow mountains: now the sun shone brightly, now it snowed," Huang Zhen wrote. "Sometimes it stormed or hailed. Hailstones were often so big that they could actually kill people."

HUANG ZHEN

In June 1935 the First Front Army began the trek over the Great Snow Mountains. As the paths grew steeper and the snow deeper, the pace dropped to six or seven hours a day.

The Jiajin range was the worst hurdle. "Rivers in full spate had to be forded, dense virgin forests and treacherous mountains crossed," Li De recalled. "The sparse population was made up of … national minorities … [who] lay in wait to ambush small groups and stragglers. Increasingly, our route was lined by the bodies of the slain … all of us were unbelievably lice-ridden. Bleeding dysentery was rampant; the first case of typhus appeared."

Long March veteran Wang Daojin said their guides sometimes made mistakes. "After walking a whole night, we found we were still walking around the same mountain," he recalled later. "We didn't dare to use electric light because we were afraid to be bombed by [GMD] planes."

Party founder Dong Biwu remembered the brutal freezing cold: "As we climbed higher, we were caught in a terrible hailstorm and the air became so thin we could hardly breathe. Speech was

impossible … Men and animals staggered and fell into chasms and disappeared … Those who sat down to rest or relieve themselves froze to death on the spot."

Troops from the southern provinces were the hardest hit. They were forced to change their diet from rice to chingko, a highland barley, causing stomach disorders. Zhou Enlai, ill with hepatitis and wracked by a cough, had to be carried on a stretcher.

The search for the Fourth Front Army became even more urgent. General Peng Dehuai led one regiment ahead in an effort to establish contact. Called to arms by Tibetan war trumpets, hostile tribes rolled boulders down on his soldiers. But after two days' marching, the First Front Army troops spotted movement across a mountain valley.

"We had started building a pontoon across a river when we suddenly saw a column of men running down toward us from the hills on the far side," recalled a First Front officer. "They were shouting to us, but the roar of the river drowned their voices. Then they threw us messages wrapped around stones, with the names of their army commanders so we could know who they were."

In the town of Maogong (known as Xiaojin today), the two armies held a great rally through the night of June 14. From its superior provisions the Fourth Front Army provided food and drink for the celebration.

Mao spoke about unity and the need to fight Japanese forces poised to flood into northern China. Li Xiannian, a Red Army captain who ultimately became China's president, remembered the unrestrained joy: "I can't begin to describe the atmosphere."

ABOVE The Red Army faced numerous hardships as it crossed the Great Snow Mountains. For the soldiers who had come from the warm and humid areas of southeastern China, the heavy snowfalls and freezing temperatures of the mountains must have been particularly harsh.
CHINA NATIONAL MUSEUM

RIGHT Red Army commander-in-chief Zhu De said the Great Snow Mountains and the Great Grasslands reduced the once-great revolutionary force to "only a skeleton."
PEOPLE'S LIBERATION ARMY PHOTO ARCHIVE

LEFT As the Communist forces struggled across rivers and through mountain passes, they had to carry most of their heavy equipment on their backs. It was an enormous job: when the Red Army began the Long March, they set out with more than 30,000 pistols, rifles and machine guns, 38 mortars and a handful of artillery pieces.

PEOPLE'S LIBERATION ARMY PHOTO ARCHIVE

ABOVE After the misery of the Great Snow Mountains, the First Front Army finally had something to celebrate when an advance party encountered the Fourth Front Army at this river crossing. The hill between them was steep and treacherous, so Fourth Army troops lowered one of their generals by rope to greet the First Front regiment..

WUQI LONG MARCH VICTORY MUSEUM

CHAPTER 6

The Treacherous Grasslands

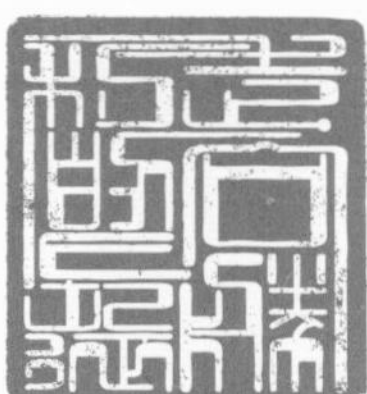

The 80,000 new comrades from the Fourth Front Army brought fresh hope to the battered First Front Army. The difference between the two groups was marked. Mao's army "looked more like beggars, wearing all kinds of clothes," a female soldier recalled. One of Mao's men remembered being impressed by the Fourth's "full uniform, with smart belts." His first glimpse of the well-fed General Zhang Guotao shocked him: "He didn't look like a Red Army commander; more like a landlord."

Soon a leadership struggle developed between two strong personalities—Mao and Zhang. Mao wanted to continue the push northward and base the combined Red Army units across Sichuan, Gansu and Shaanxi provinces. After some debate, Zhang proposed establishing a base in border regions to the south, closer to help that might come from the Soviet Union.

LEFT This hand-colored glass plate photograph from the 1940s leaves no doubt about how perilous the Great Grasslands were. Despite the awe-inspiring beauty of the landscape, it was a place of almost unceasing misery for the Long Marchers, with soldiers, horses and supplies disappearing in icy bogs of black mud.
YAN'AN REVOLUTIONARY MUSEUM

BELOW Dong Zhentang led the 5th Army Corps of the First Front Army, which provided rearguard protection on the Long March. "He was alert, calm, firm and brave during battle, a good example for army commanders," Huang Zhen wrote. "He always carried his pistol with him and had a habit of standing with one hand on his hip while holding a short pole in the other hand."

HUANG ZHEN

To break the impasse, Zhu De proposed a compromise: move north to secure the nearest areas of Gansu province before the GMD could get there, then establish a unified headquarters with himself as commander-in-chief and Zhang Guotao as commissar.

Mao reluctantly agreed. The combined First and Fourth armies would continue north, with Mao leading columns on the right, Zhang on the left. Ahead lay yet another barrier, completely different from the Great Snow Mountains but in many ways no less terrifying—the Great Grasslands.

As the Long Marchers soon learned, the term is a highly misleading euphemism. On the Sichuan–Gansu border some 12,000 feet (3,600 meters) above sea level, vast swathes of grassy tundra cover hidden bogs, capable of swallowing men and animals whole. The conditions were not suited to agriculture, so food was scarce.

Mao's vanguard pushed into the Grasslands on August 21, 1935. With supplies dwindling, the army was forced to institute strict rationing. Troops often subsisted on boiled grass flavored with salt. Everyone was weak; many starved to death. Mao suffered another bout of malaria, which he had contracted on the eve of his departure from Jiangxi. Zhou, running a high fever, was carried on a stretcher.

"A deceptive green cover hid a black viscous swamp, which sucked in anyone who broke through the thin crust or strayed from the narrow path," Li De wrote of the pitiless terrain.

"We drove native cattle or horses before us, which instinctively found the least dangerous way … Cold rain fell several times a day and at night turned to wet snow or sleet. There was not a dwelling, tree or shrub as far as the eye could see. We slept in squatting positions … Some did not waken in the morning, victims of cold and exhaustion."

One Long March veteran recalled conditions worse than anything the First Front Army had experienced: "Soldiers following behind covered up those who died. Some about to die had hearts still beating, but we had to cover them, too—or at least their faces, otherwise it was too ugly."

Another survivor remembered, above all, the hunger: "When we came out of those marshes, we began eating rats. We cleaned every village of rats."

The Red Army lost more troops during the week-long crossing of the Grasslands than it did on the trek across the Great Snow Mountains. Some 40,000 men marched with Mao on the eastern route; 10,000 did not come out. A Nationalist army tried to follow the Communists into the Grasslands but soon turned back.

The GMD, however, were not yet finished with the hunt. Ahead of the revolutionaries lay the Minshan mountain range, a barrier between north Sichuan and south Gansu. The only feasible way through was via the Lazikou Pass, a passage just 100 feet (30 meters) wide with an almost perpendicular cliff rising more than 1,000 feet (300 meters) to one side.

ABOVE As the Red Army made its way across the Great Grasslands, troops saw nothing but high grassy swamp land—no trees, no insects, no birds, no stones. For peasant boys from China's fertile south such a desolate landscape affected morale. The eerie landscape was described by one veteran as a "nether world."

PEOPLE'S LIBERATION ARMY PHOTO ARCHIVE

FOLLOWING PAGES Although paintings like this intended to show the tenacious spirit of the Long March revolutionaries as they crossed the Great Grasslands, the terrain behind the troops illustrates how difficult and at times disheartening the crossing must have been.

WUQI LONG MARCH VICTORY MUSEUM

LEFT The Red Army carried boards with the words to songs, which they sang to keep spirits up as they marched and to spread the Communist message to local people. This one reads: "We grow the crops, but the rich people use them to cook their soup. The landlords and the rich live in mansions, but the peasant and the farmer live in huts. Plus we have to pay lots of tax. They suck our lifeblood. Only when you join the Red Army and win the battle will you free yourself from this oppression."

CHINA NATIONAL MUSEUM

RIGHT This photo shows the place where the Red Army fought their way through the Lazikou Pass. The road on the right was built by blasting into the hillside, but at the time of the Long March, troops made their way along a narrow path, making combat very difficult.

MICHAEL YOUNG

It was an ideal place for the the Nationalists to finally block the Long March.

In an encounter with a GMD division the Red Army had taken some prisoners who revealed that the Nationalists had built some of their infamous "turtle shells" at Lazikou Pass—the same circular blockhouses that had given the Red Army so much trouble a year earlier in Jiangxi province.

The Red Army faced a terrifying dilemma: get through Lazikou or return to the horrors of the Great Grasslands. The order was given: "We must take the Pass!"

On the afternoon of September 15, 1935, the Red Army launched dozens of assaults against Lazikou. Troops tried to scramble up cliffside paths linked by swinging log bridges, all the while raked by GMD machine-gun fire. But the terrain and the "turtle shells" prevailed. Faced with terrible, continuing losses, Mao called a halt at midnight.

When the attack resumed, a young political commissar led a company of troops in a nighttime frontal assault, while two other companies launched flanking movements around Lazikou's fortifications—a sortie on the right and, after a climb down the steep mountain cliff, an assault from the rear. A band of

ABOVE As the Long March continued, tobacco became more and more difficult to find. Troops discovered a passable substitute in the Grasslands, a local grass that could be dried and smoked. It had, in the words of Huang Zhen, "a different taste."

HUANG ZHEN

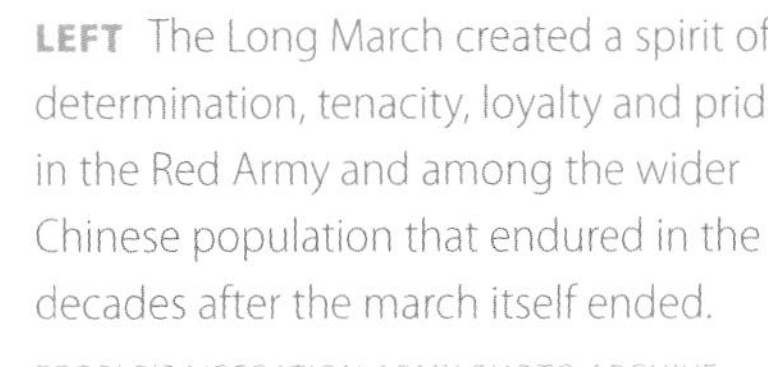

LEFT The Long March created a spirit of determination, tenacity, loyalty and pride in the Red Army and among the wider Chinese population that endured in the decades after the march itself ended.
PEOPLE'S LIBERATION ARMY PHOTO ARCHIVE

ABOVE Yaks, common on the Tibetan plateau, would have been an excellent source of milk, meat and hide for clothes and tents. However, as Huang Zhen pointed out, troops had to catch them first. "It is not an easy job to capture a wild yak," he wrote. "Usually people do not dare to offend it. Once offended, it might rush madly at you with the strength to overturn a truck."
HUANG ZHEN

experienced mountaineers—more than 30 men, including about 12 tribesmen from the Miao minority—had been selected for this arduous assignment.

One volunteer wrapped his body in explosives, leaped from the cliff into the middle of the Nationalist concentrations and blew himself up. In the face of such determination, the enemy panicked, many throwing away their guns and fleeing.

Mao's central army, broken in health but not in spirit, marched north through Gansu province.

CHAPTER 7

The Last Steps to Shaanxi

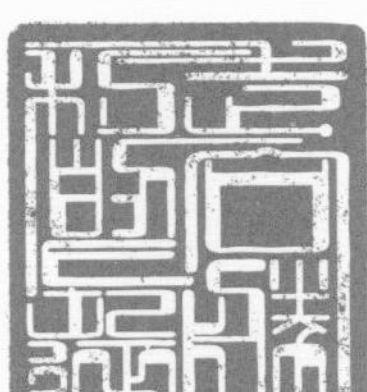

The First Front Army now began the last of its countless slogs across the face of China. Even in late September 1935, Mao had no precise destination for his troops. The terrain in this part of Gansu province is extremely difficult—narrow, circuitous paths through hillsides ready to fall away. But at the Red Army's first stop—mid-morning September 21, 1935, in the village of Hadapu—Mao decided that it was time to celebrate.

It was the first ethnic Han town they had encountered since their passage through Yunnan four months earlier. From the cash reserves lugged across mountains and through swamps each soldier was handed two silver dollars. Mao made a speech that concluded, "Everyone should eat well."

Soldiers found a nine-day-old copy of *Ta Kung Pao*, a national newspaper. Clamorous headlines alleged GMD forces were suppressing "Red bandits" in northern Shaanxi provinces, the first confirmation of rumors that Red Army units were active nearby. The papers revealed that Mao's friend, Liu Zhidan, commander of the 26th Army Corps, and Xu Haidong of the 25th Army Corps were still alive.

LEFT Hadapu's Ming-era old town, with its cobblestone streets and red-walled buildings, remains largely unchanged from the time the First Front Army stopped there in 1935.

HAROLD WELDON

BELOW Boards with proclamations from the Red Army were posted in every town and village the revolutionaries passed through. This one reads: "The Red Army are the troops of the workers and the peasants. We guarantee that we will look after and protect the interests of all ethnic groups, Miao, Muslim, Yi and Tibetan."

CHINA NATIONAL MUSEUM

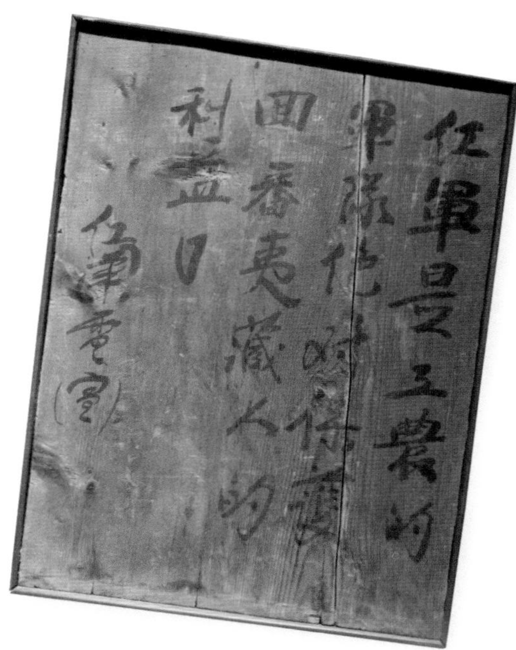

Zhou Enlai set up his headquarters in Hadapu's Buddhist temple, and the leaders conferred. They decided that the First Front Army now had a firm objective: march toward northern Shaanxi. Mao stressed the threat from what he called "a gray dragon"—the Japanese army. His orders: "Complete the march to the north and fight the Japanese occupiers!"

The Red Army marched on until October 19, 1935, when it reached Wuqi, where Shaanxi's Communist units came to meet them and act as guides. At area headquarters Liu Zhidan and Xu Haidong greeted them with a crowd joyously beating gongs.

For Mao and the few thousand ragged survivors of the First Front Army, the Long March—after 368 days of marching and fighting, covering an average of 18.8 miles (30.3 kilometers) a day—had effectively ended.

The marching continued for other Red Army units for another year. Still convinced that there were better places to regroup than remote Shaanxi and still seeking to replace Mao as leader, Zhang Guotao had Fourth Front Army elements establish bases in western Sichuan and on the rich plains northeast of Chengdu, Sichuan's provincial capital.

At first, the expedition seemed to go well. But then Nationalist forces gained the upper hand and Zhang was forced to move westward to Ganzi near Xizang (Tibet), an inhospitable region with unfriendly inhabitants. There they suffered crushing losses at the hands of GMD-allied warlord Ma Bufang.

In November 1935, He Long's Second Front Army, which included Xiao Ke's elite 6th Army Corps, started westward on their own, subsidiary Long March. After spending some time in Guizhou,

LEFT When Fourth Front Army troops got to Huining, in Gansu province, they were greeted by a slogan painted next to the town gates by First Front Army soldiers who had arrived earlier. It read: "Keep moving on and keep strong."
WUQI LONG MARCH VICTORY MUSEUM

BELOW Zhou Enlai, who endured hardship and life-threatening illness on the Long March, finally made it to northern Shaanxi.
YAN'AN REVOLUTIONARY MUSEUM

they pushed southwest into Yunnan, crossed the Golden Sands River, then headed north toward Ganzi. In the summer of 1936 they joined up with the remnants of the Fourth Front Army.

The armies marched to Huining, Gansu province, where Mao and the First Front Army were waiting. At last the three great arms of the Red Army—the First Front, the Second Front and the Fourth Front—had come together. "The Red Armies' union heralds peace for China," Mao declared.

The Long March officially ended on October 22, 1936. At a grand celebration in front of Huining's Confucian Temple, commander-in-chief Zhu De read out a telegram from the CCP's central committee: "The union of the three main Red Armies and their entrance into the anti-Japanese front line will be crucial … we will fight to safeguard … the whole of China."

"The darkest time in our history was during the Long March—especially when we crossed the Great Grasslands," Zhou Enlai said many years later. "Our condition was desperate. We not only had nothing to eat, we had nothing to drink. Yet we survived ..."

BELOW Huang Zhen said that, when the Red Army marched into Hadapu, the local people greeted them "as if we were their own family."
HUANG ZHEN

Mao decided to create a permanent base in Yan'an, a minor market town in northern Shaanxi. No longer distracted by challenges from Zhang, who defected to the GMD in 1937, Mao made sure that his position as supreme leader was no longer in doubt.

It was Mao himself who gave the revolutionaries' two-year ordeal the name by which it is now remembered. In a speech in December 1935 to a CCP conference in northern Shaanxi, he used the term "Long March" for the first time.

"Let us ask, has history ever known a long march to equal ours? No, never!" Mao declared. "The Long March is a manifesto. It has proclaimed to the world that the Red Army is an army of heroes, while the imperialists and their running dogs, Chiang Kai-shek and his like, are impotent."

* * *

It is a curious military truth that retreat often brings out the best in a nation. Ancient Greece took comfort from the story of 10,000 young men who unsuccessfully invaded the Persian empire in 401 BC and spent the next two years fighting their way back home. And the British still recall with pride the "Miracle of Dunkirk," when an armada of little ships crossed the English Channel in 1940 to rescue 330,000 Allied troops facing certain defeat at the hands of German forces.

BELOW This photograph, taken in Yan'an at or near the end of the Long March, captures the young soldiers of the Red Army in a relaxed and informal moment.
PEOPLE'S LIBERATION ARMY PHOTO ARCHIVE

RIGHT This painting commemorates the moment Mao led the First Front Army into Wuqi, Shaanxi province, in October 1935. For Mao, the punishing slog through the wilds of China was over, though the Long March didn't officially end until the arrival of the Second Front Army and the Fourth Front Army in October 1936.

CHINA NATIONAL MUSEUM

RIGHT These young troops, shown on parade in Yan'an around 1940, carried the spirit and tradition of the Long March into the Sino-Japanese War.

PEOPLE'S LIBERATION ARMY PHOTO ARCHIVE

As a demonstration of solidarity and endurance, however, few retreats can match the Long March. Mao's spirited leadership and his ability to mobilize a downtrodden peasantry in the face of a much stronger enemy gave new life to the emerging revolution. It was the beginning of a New China.

When Mao wrote his famous poem "The Long March" just weeks after arriving exhausted in northern Shaanxi, he evoked the sense of good fortune that had favored the courageous and tenacious Red Army. It was a feeling of triumph over adversity, of nothing to fear but more to do.

The Red Army fears not the
trials of the March,
Holding light ten thousand
crags and torrents.
The Five Ridges wind like
gentle ripples,
And the majestic Wumeng rolls
by, globules of clay.
Warm the steep cliffs lapped by
the waters of Golden Sand,
Cold the iron chains spanning
the Dadu River.
Minshan's thousand li of snow
joyously crossed,
The three Armies march on,
each face glowing.

The Red Army had walked and fought over 6,000 miles (10,000 kilometers), crossing 24 mighty rivers and 18 major mountain ranges (five covered with snow) across 11 provinces through some of the world's most difficult and unforgiving terrain. Only one in twenty Red Army soldiers had survived.

As Mao proclaimed: "We were under daily reconnaissance and bombing from the air by scores of planes, we were encircled, pursued, obstructed and intercepted on the ground by a big force of several hundred thousand men … we encountered untold difficulties and great obstacles on the way, but by keeping our two feet going we swept across … the length and breadth of China."

The Long March was a victory of the human spirit and a testament to the strength and willpower of the men and women who took part. The survival, triumph and unity of purpose of the

ABOVE By the time the Long March ended in 1936, Mao Zedong and Zhu De had been comrades-in-arms for nearly a decade. But in many ways, the work of these war-weary leaders had just begun. The Red Army would go on to fight the invading Japanese before finally vanquishing Chiang Kai-shek's Nationalist government in 1949.
YAN'AN REVOLUTIONARY MUSEUM

Long Marchers would become the foundation on which the revolution, and eventual proclamation of the People's Republic of China in October 1949, was formed.

In the years since, the Long March has endured as a symbol of strength and achievement. Stories of the march have given successive Chinese generations a benchmark for courage, determination and achievement. Schools present Long March awards to students for improving their marks, and outstanding workers in government and private industry receive

New Long March Pacesetter awards. The phrase has even entered the world of commerce. "Long March" is used as a brand name on a vast range of Chinese products, including rubber tires, pharmaceuticals and computers.

But for any soldier who marched with Mao, surely the most appealing use of the name is the family of rockets produced by China's Academy of Launch Vehicle Technology. In 1970, a Long March rocket carried the Dong Fang Hong ("East Is Red") satellite into orbit, making China the fifth nation to enter the space race. In 2008, Long March 2F carried Shenzhou 7, China's first three-man mission, into orbit. Advanced Long March rockets are expected to put Chinese astronauts on the moon by about 2015 and on Mars by about 2040.

According to the official record, the Long March ended October 22, 1936. But in a very real sense the march continues for China. The entry into space is a journey that, literally, has no end. The Long March seems destined to go on forever.

ABOVE After the Long March, Mao returned to Zunyi for a reunion with his comrades from the Jinggangshan revolutionary base, which had served as the Red Army's headquarters in the late 1920s before they moved to Jiangxi province.

ZUNYI CONFERENCE MEMORIAL MUSEUM

FOLLOWING PAGES With the Long March over, the Red Army established its new base in Yan'an and turned its energies to fighting the Japanese. These soldiers, proudly wearing their Red Army caps on parade at the Yan'an revolutionary base, were replenished and ready for deployment .

YAN'AN REVOLUTIONARY MUSEUM

THE LONG MARCH CONTINUES

CHAPTER 8

The Great Transformation

Much of the story of China since the Long March has been told in terms of battles, revolutions and upheavals: the Sino-Japanese War, the creation of the People's Republic, the Great Leap Forward, the Cultural Revolution. More recently, the story has become one of the emergence of a strong market economy.

Over the past three decades, China has undergone the greatest industrial revolution ever seen, starting slowly at first, then accelerating with breathtaking speed. The transformation is so deep and profound it could rightly be called the New Long March.

Fittingly, some of the most dramatic changes are happening along and near the path of the original Long March. Without question, this part of China had a long way to go. As Mao Zedong's soldiers retreated westward, then northward, few parts of the world were as remote or primitive. At the Dadu River, scene of one of the Long March's most decisive battles, the local Yi people greeted the Red Army in a state of almost total nudity. Another minority tribe in this area worshipped snakes. Squalor and illiteracy were the locals' lot.

LEFT In much of western China, traditional ways and modern development exist side by side. On this road north of Yan'an in Shaanxi province, a local farmer and his wife head to market.
SONG GANGMING

In a sense, the Long March planted the seeds of the coming transformation, even if change came very slowly at first. "Like an involuntary and monumental study tour, [the Long March] splendidly completed the revolutionaries' already unrivaled knowledge of the Chinese peasants' psychology," French author Tibor Mende wrote following a visit to China in 1960. "It brought them into contact with new regions and different peoples. Disseminating their ideas among them on their way, they also learned a great deal about the problems and attitudes of masses they were destined to govern later on."

Following the Communist victory in 1949, Mao had to put aside his enthusiasm for the western regions and made the well-being of the huge urban populations in the east his first order of business. But he had not forgotten the interior. In a speech to party cadres in April 1956 he noted that 70 percent of China's industry was located in coastal regions, and only 30 percent in the interior. "This irrational situation is a product of history," he declared. The "greater part of new industry should be located in the interior so that industry may gradually become more evenly distributed."

LEFT In Xinduqiao, Ganzi Tibetan Autonomous Prefecture, this ethnic Tibetan couple uses traditional construction techniques to build a new house, one stone at a time.
SHI YONGTING

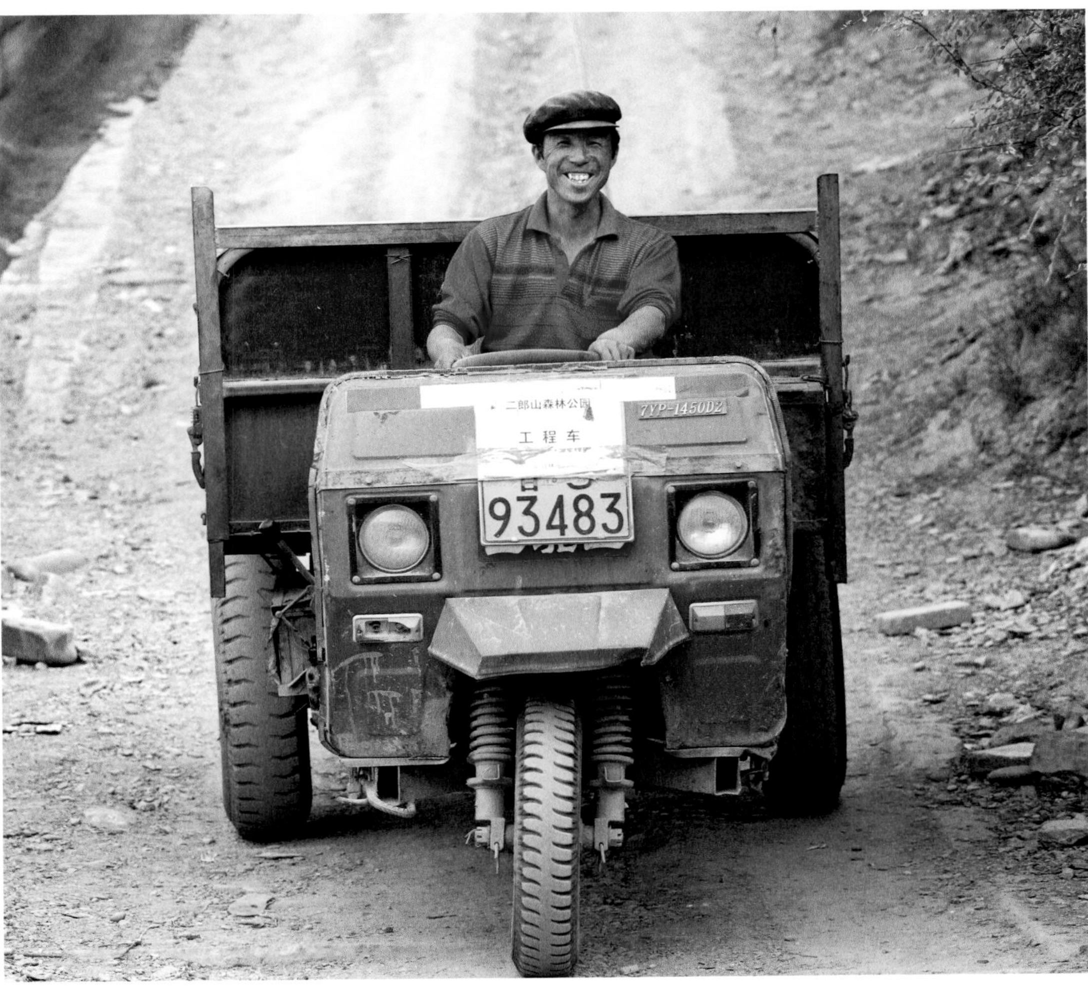

BELOW In the rush to build a modern China, the country's history has not been forgotten. This worker is part of a team rebuilding an ancient temple in the town of Minxian, Gansu province.
MICHAEL YOUNG

Unlike other great national expansions, such as the settlement of the American West in the 19th century, China's westward push was driven not by individual pioneers but largely by the government. To keep beyond the enemy's reach during the Sino-Japanese War, Chiang Kai-shek moved the Nationalist government and much of its military production to Chongqing from 1939 to 1945.

And Mao, also fearing the threat posed by outsiders, ordered that substantial sections of the country's industrial base—power generation, and aviation and electronic manufacturing—be moved to the southwest and west in the late 1950s. The Chinese high command spoke about the coast and the northeastern frontier as the "first front line" and the central regions as the "second line." Sichuan, Guizhou,

FOLLOWING PAGES Massive rail and road systems, such as this one in Jiangxi province, crisscross much of western China. The Shanghai–Kunming line, which passes through Jiangxi, was upgraded in 2006, allowing trains to travel at speeds up to 120 miles (200 kilometers) per hour.
LIU SHAONING

LEFT Modern technologies like solar panels have allowed ethnic Tibetans to maintain their traditonal summer grazing by providing amenities like electricity. This family lives in a tent in the grasslands outside of the town of Rou'ergai in the far north of Sichuan province.
LEO MEIER

Yunnan and other inland provinces were the "third line."

Over the decades the People's Liberation Army has run its own businesses as a way of reducing its reliance on state funds. More recently, in the past decade or so, the PLA has been converting many of these commercial enterprises into private companies. Numerous examples can be found today in western China. Sichuan, for example, is the site of no fewer than 79 former military enterprises.

The Changhong Electronics Group in western Sichuan is now China's largest manufacturer of television sets and a large exporter of car and motorbike parts. Chongqing Changan Automobile Group, China's fourth largest carmaker, is descended from a "third line" enterprise that assembled military jeeps with the brand name Yangzi.

Despite some advances, however, concerns lingered about the economic imbalance between eastern and western China. Economists Hu Angang and Wang Shaoguang wrote in a 1993 essay: "If China were to wait [before developing poorer areas, especially in its west], the disparity between regions might eventually become too sharp to be resolved; if income gaps were allowed to widen, catastrophic political consequences might ensue.

中国
台，是您施展才华的天地，
新法，发挥点石成金的魔力，
汗水耕耘，
了祖国的花朵更加绚丽，
深夜，您批改作业，
陪伴您的是爱人的鼾声，
明，您撰写教案，
您的是孩子的梦呓，
片映红东方的朝霞，
擎起旭日
熠熠生辉的红
燃烧自己。

我们爱您

LEFT Two young singers from the Shaanxi Cultural Performance Troupe perform a romantic love song in Ansai county, north of Yan'an. The Ansai region has a long tradition of folk singing and dancing.
MICHAEL YOUNG

Accordingly … China must make serious efforts to narrow the regional gap and at a minimum prevent them from growing." Hu and Wang pointed out that both the Soviet Union and Yugoslavia had recently broken up in part due to regional inequalities within each country.

Beijing took note of the imbalance between the increasingly affluent eastern regions and the often-struggling provinces in the west. The Great Western Development Strategy was unveiled in 1999 with the goal of transforming the economy and living standards of western China—most notably Gansu, Guangxi, Guizhou, Qinghai, Shaanxi, Sichuan and Yunnan.

Over the past decade, the central government has committed hundreds of billions of dollars to the strategy, with the promise of much more to come. In the west, southwest and northwest more than 500 significant development projects are underway or are in the planning stages. They include the West–East Gas Pipeline Project; 10,500 miles (17,000 kilometers) of the 5 North–South and 7 East–West national highway grid; the Chongqing–Huaihua and Xi'an–Nanjing railroads; airport construction in Xi'an, Chengdu, Kunming, Lanzhou and Urumqi; an elevated light rail in Chongqing; irrigation works at Sichuan's Zipingu and Ningxia's Shapotou hydroelectric power and dam projects; and extensive reforestation and pasture recovery projects. The list goes on and on.

"By the mid-21st century, an entirely new west is expected to emerge," says Li Xiaojian, economic geography professor at Henan University and vice chairman of the China Geographical Society.

A central plank of the Western Development Strategy is a dramatic increase in electricity capacity,

BELOW Signs of a modern and lively economy can be seen just about everywhere. Here a couple of models prepare to be photographed in a rooftop advertising shoot in the town of Minxian.
MICHAEL YOUNG

PREVIOUS PAGES These young students are hard at work at a primary school in the Danba area, Sichuan province. The sign behind them says: "China, we love you." In all, China has 300,000 primary schools with over 17 million students.
LI FAN

FOLLOWING PAGES The town of Dong Chuan, in northeastern Yunnan province, sits at the foot of the Wumeng mountains. The Red Army passed through the mountains during the Long March, and they were later immortalized in the poem "The Long March" by Mao Zedong: "And the majestic Wumeng roll by, globules of clay." Today the area is a popular tourist destination, thanks to its beautiful scenery, rich red soil and dramatic skies.
HEI MING

ABOVE Ciping Limei Ren, an 80-year-old tailor in Jinggangshan, Jiangxi province, assembles a Red Army uniform. Replica uniforms are popular among tourists who retrace the Long March on the so-called "Red Tour." These tourists often wear replica uniforms for photographs and as a sign of respect for Long March soldiers.
LIU SHAONING

particularly through hydroelectric projects. Today China is the world's leader in hydroelectricity capacity, much of it generated by large-scale dams in the west. Yunnan and Sichuan each have 18 large dams. The Changheba Dam and Dagangshan Dam are being built on the Dadu River. Near the site of the battle for the Luding Bridge, a 180-mile (300-kilometer) complex of underground tunnels and channels will soon be drawing water from the Dadu, Jinsha and Yalong rivers.

The focus on hydroelectricity is part of a drive to develop sustainable energy that will reduce pollution generated by China's heavy reliance on coal. As a Chinese University of Hong Kong study puts it: "Despite the fact that the West possesses over 74% of China's hydropower potential, only 8% of it has been developed, whereas the East is endowed with only 7% of the potential, and yet 50% has been developed."

The West–East Gas Pipeline is also helping the battle against pollution. Four

separate lines costing more than US$30 billion pump gas from as far away as Sichuan and Xinjiang in China and from wells as distant as Myanmar and Turkmenistan to users in the east and southeast. Low-pollution gas from the completed pipelines now accounts for 8 percent of China's energy supply.

"The project is the centerpiece of China's … program to develop the west," says Professor Y.M. Yeung, director of the Shanghai–Hong Kong Development Institute.

ABOVE These Sichuan farmers are collecting "wo sun" asparagus lettuce, a popular Chinese green vegetable.
RICHARD MCLAREN

FOLLOWING PAGES Trucks haul raw white marble, close to Baoxing County. This part of Sichuan is also famous for another natural wonder: the first recorded sightings of giant pandas happened in the area in 1869, and the animals are now protected in the Sichuan Giant Panda Sanctuaries.
RICHARD MCLAREN

Two other cornerstones of this new era in the west are communications and digital technology. A Chinese University of Hong Kong study says China has entered "a new age predicated upon the production, acquisition and transmission of new information, hence the name Information Age or the New Economy."

Data from China's National Bureau of Statistics details the remarkable growth of communications infrastructure over the past decade. Between 2003 and 2009, the number of fixed-line telephones has grown by almost 20 percent to 314 million, while the number of mobile phone users has nearly tripled to 747 million.

China has by far the world's biggest online population. Nearly half a billion Chinese were using the Internet regularly in 2011, and that number is forecast to grow to 812 million by 2015.

Much of the action in the information technology sector is happening in the west. Intel, the world's largest chip-maker, has invested US$525 million in two assembly and testing facilities in Chengdu, Sichuan's capital. Motorola has established an R&D center for

LEFT A Yi nationality farmer in the village of Anshun, Sichuan province, where part of the Red Army crossed the Dadu River during the Long March. Support from local Yi tribesmen was a key element of the Red Army's survival in this rugged and hostile area.
LIANG DAMING

mobile telecommunications in Sichuan, while Nokia, Sony, Motorola, Microsoft, Ericsson, Cisco, Texas Instruments and IBM have all made substantial investments in the province. Chengdu factories owned by the Foxconn Technology Group of Taiwan now produce half of the world's iPads.

In 2010 Hewlett-Packard began manufacturing notebook computers in Chongqing. "Our goal is to expand Chongqing's IT industry into one worth RMB 1 trillion (US$149 billion), accounting for 40 percent of the city's total industry by 2015," declares Mu Huaping, director of the Chongqing Economic and Information Technology Commission.

An extraordinarily important page in history has begun to turn. The original Long March started the process of bringing much of China's interior into the modern era, and huge investments in these areas over the past decade are helping to turn the country into an economic powerhouse. Tsinghua University economist Dr. Hu Angang, who back in 1993 was among the first people to call for greater development in western China, believes the payoff will come in the next decade.

In his book, *China in 2020: A New Type of Superpower*, Hu says China will in all likelihood "not only surpass the United States as the world's largest economy but also (because of its accomplishments in education, innovation and clean energy) emerge as a mature, responsible and attractive superpower.

"History is now providing China with the same opportunity to thrive that the United States enjoyed between 1871 and 1913, Japan between 1955 and 1988, and Korea between 1965 and 1996."

BELOW The Jinggangshan Reservoir dam in Jiangxi province is just one of more than 25,000 hydroelectric dams found throughout China. The Jinggangshan dam is a double curvature arch structure with a generating capacity of 12 megawatts.
MICHAEL YOUNG

RIGHT The Long March continues to touch the lives of people along the route. Wang Xiaoqian has her wedding photos taken at the Tagong Temple in Tagong Village, in western Sichuan, to honour the memory of her grandfather, who passed through the area on the Long March.

LI FAN

FOLLOWING PAGES This newly constructed town will house over 100,000 people whose villages were flooded following the construction of a series of dams along the Dadu River. The dams are part of both a hydroelectric power program and a scheme to divert water from the Dadu River to the Yellow River in the north of China.

MICHAEL YOUNG

CHAPTER 9

Change in the Jiangxi Circle

The Red Army's decision to pull out of Jiangxi in 1934 reflected a stark reality: if they stayed and continued to fight Chiang Kai-shek's Fifth Encirclement Campaign, they would be wiped out. Retreat equaled survival. The Long March was launched on this simple equation.

For a brief while, Jiangxi and Fujian benefited from being at the center of the action. During the Encirclement Campaign in 1933 and 1934, the Nationalists built more than 5,000 miles (8,000 kilometers) of roads and an equal length of telephone lines. It was an unusual burst of activity for an area largely run by feckless warlords more interested in opium-trafficking, brothels and slave markets than in building modern infrastructure.

After the Red Army departed, Jiangxi and Fujian remained outside China's mainstream for many years. That started to change in the 1960s, when Mao Zedong, concerned that a world war could be imminent, ordered the urgent transfer of strategic industries to interior provinces. Jiangxi became the site for production of the 09 series of nuclear-powered attack submarines.

LEFT The rice harvest has begun in the Jinggangshan rural area in eastern Jiangxi. With so many mouths to feed, food security is a major issue in China. The country produced 500 million tons of rice in 2008, and this number will grow to an estimated 630 million tons by 2020.
LIU SHAONING

BELOW This modern basketball stadium in Ruijin new town can hold more than 1,000 people. The sport has become hugely popular in China in recent decades, with 300 million people now playing basketball. It was first played at universities, but today China has professional basketball leagues for men and women, and Chinese players have found success overseas, most notably Yao Ming in the American National Basketball Association.

LIU SHAONING

The area's fortunes truly started to improve when Deng Xiaoping, who had been sent from Beijing to work in a Jiangxi tractor factory during the Cultural Revolution, became China's paramount leader. As the Yangzi valley opened to foreign trade and investment under Deng's policies of economic liberalization, Jiangxi's annual growth quickly outpaced the national average. It was one of the first provinces to contribute to China's transformation into "the world's assembly line." Other production centers in the region—Guangdong, Guangxi, Fujian—followed suit.

Today, evidence of this growth can be found throughout Jiangxi. The shipyards that once assembled warships now build freighters, electronics and industrial machinery. Thanks to massive investment in the province's mines, Jiangxi now has six of China's largest copper mines.

Transportation infrastructure is also improving. The Beijing–Kowloon Railway, opened in 1996, now connects with the Hangzhou–Nanchang Railway in Jiangxi; more than 140 trains travel this line on a daily basis.

More recently, ambitious senior party officials in southern provinces have been working on a plan to integrate the economies of the Pearl River Delta by demolishing administrative barriers

Visiting historical sites along the route of the Long March on "Red Tours" is becoming increasingly popular. Ruijin alone attracts more than 1.3 million tourists every year.

BELOW Residents of Ruijin gather at a local shop to watch a video of the Chinese opera *Gan Nan Cai Cha*. The shop's owner (left) takes time to greet and joke with the audience before the show begins.
LIU SHAONING

LEFT Fried snack bars abound in the streets of Ruijin and throughout Jiangxi, offering such dishes as dried bean curd, sausages, vegetables, kelp rolls, cutlets and banana or lotus root slices. At this stall in Xingguo county, a woman is making the local dish *shao yu le*—fish that has been rolled in flour and fried.
LIU SHAONING

between Jiangxi, Fujian, Guangdong, Guangxi, Guizhou, Hainan, Hunan, Sichuan and Yunnan.

In a speech in Jiangxi, during his celebrated tour of southern China in 1992, Deng Xiaoping highlighted the strategic importance of the region's production of rare earth metals. "The Middle East has its oil, China has rare earth: 80 percent of identified global resources," he declared. "You can compare the status of those reserves to that of oil in the Middle East."

Today, China is responsible for more than 90 percent of all rare earth metal production. These metals—especially europium, lanthanum, praseodymium, cerium and samarium—are a vital part of the manufacture of such products as tablet computers, fluorescent lightbulbs, wind turbines, jet engines, gasoline–electric hybrid cars, DVD drives and TV monitors.

China mines 120,000 tons per year, followed by the United States (about 5,000 tons) and India (2,700 tons). Jiangxi is China's main producer of medium and heavy rare metals, used to make camera lenses, oil refining equipment, high refractive index glass and battery electrodes. Beijing seems determined to strengthen its grip on production of rare metals, much of which is reportedly smuggled abroad. For example, Jiangxi's 88 licenses for

rare earth mines are being consolidated in a singe mega-license, making export easier to control.

According to legend, the northern Jiangxi city of Jingdezhen gave its name to China itself. As the story goes, Jingdezhen, long the hub of the country's porcelain industry, was once called Changnanzhen. Foreign traders found the name difficult to pronounce and shortened it to Changnan, then China. The name stuck, for both the country and its ceramics. To this day, traders and shoppers from all over visit Jingdezhen's International Trade Square market and the Ancient Kiln Folk Exhibition to buy china made by the finest ceramics masters.

Interestingly, locally mined high-quality feldspar clay, an important ingredient in ceramics, is also vital to electronic components. Aerospace and electronics factories proliferate in Jiangxi.

Neighboring Fujian has had mixed fortunes over the past half-century or so. In 1950, defeated Nationalist forces fled to Taiwan, just across the Taiwan Strait from Fujian. The province remained under tight military control, curbing trade and hampering development.

Many Fujianese emigrated during years of war and deprivation, and many of these hard workers became rich. Investment by the Fujian diaspora—and their counterparts from Guangdong and Guangxi—is now pouring into real estate, hotel and factory development.

However far Jiangxi and Fujian may be from the centers of power in Beijing and Shanghai, they cannot be called backwaters any longer.

ABOVE Souvenir shops such as the Red Well in the village of Shazhouba cater to tourists who take the "Red Tour" along the path of the Long March.
MICHAEL YOUNG

RIGHT This street, Dian Tou Jie in Chang Ting county, Fujian province, has changed little since it served as a supply base for troops on the Long March. Today visitors to the street can buy traditional handmade goods. Typically shops face the street and workshops are located in the back.
LIU SHAONING

PREVIOUS PAGES The Jinggang Longtan Waterfall is one of more than 100 waterfalls in the Jinggang Mountains. Covering 260 square miles (670 square kilometers) in Hunan and Jiangxi provinces, the Jinggang Mountains are known as the cradle of the Chinese revolution because Mao Zedong formed the first Chinese Soviet there in the late 1920s.
MICHAEL YOUNG

通仙佛具
佛像、佛龛、佛珠
念佛机、香纸蜡烛
佛事用品
纯米酒
发型设计

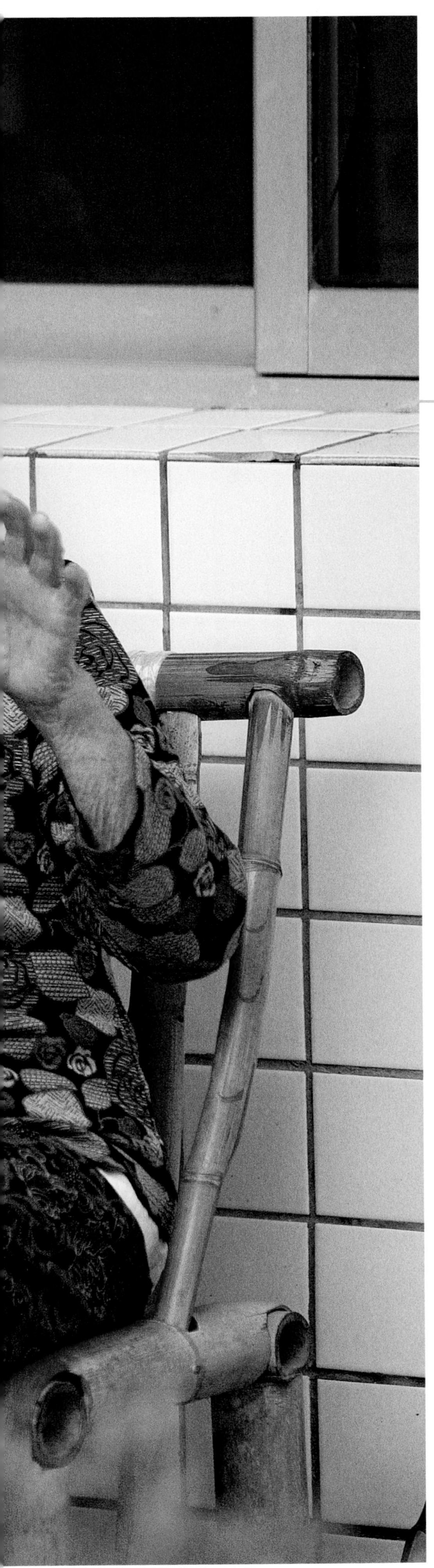

LEFT Two residents of a nursing home in Ruijin enjoy each other's company. China now has an estimated 100 million people over the age of 70. China's strong traditions of family and community are becoming more important than ever as the country deals with the challenges of an aging population.

LIU SHAONING

ABOVE The Ruijin Golden Cable Factory manufactures cross-linked power cables. While Jiangxi has gold, silver and uranium mines, its most important minerals are copper and tungsten. Copper mining rose to prominence following the discovery of vast reserves at Dexing, in the northeast of the province.

LIU SHAONING

BELOW A young boy cycles through the historic buildings that were once part of a Red Army school and medical complex in Ruijin. The sign seen through the doorway reads: "Doctor Zhong Xian."
LIU SHAONING

RIGHT A woman weaves a basket in the daily market section of the old town of Ruijin. As in much of rural China, Ruijin is undergoing great transformation as new town development rises up around the old. Despite the dramatic changes, demand for traditional skills like basket weaving remains.
LIU SHAONING

CG274

皇明
桑夏

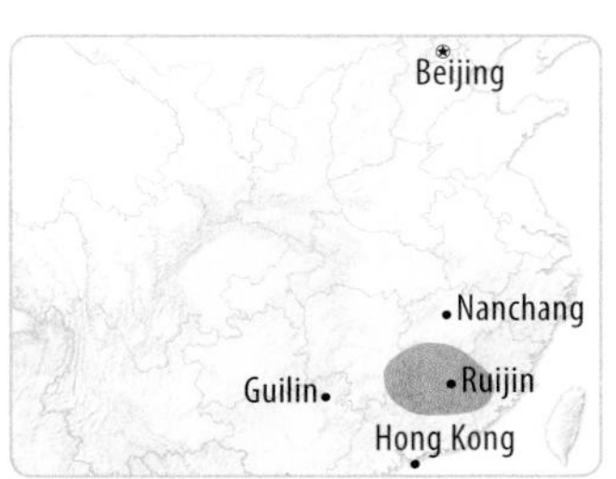

PREVIOUS PAGES With China's population growing, especially in urban areas, and incomes on the rise, demand for housing has skyrocketed. These colourful luxury villas have sprung up in the new town section of Ruijin.
LIU SHAONING

LEFT Despite the growth of Ruijin's new town, the farmers market in the old town continues to attract large crowds of shoppers by offering a wide array of fresh produce.
LIU SHAONING

ABOVE The Jiangxi Soviet's central government building in Ruijin, where much of the Communist Party was based in the years before the Long March, has been preserved as an historic site. The sign over the door says: "Temporary Central Government of China Soviet Republic."
LIU SHAONING

RIGHT Yudu County Long March Origin Primary School in Jiangxi province was named in honor of the fact that the Long March began when Red Army troops crossed the Yudu River in this area.
LIU SHAONING

FAR RIGHT As China's rapid development continues, modern industry and traditional farming are learning to live side by side, as with this cement factory near Ruijin.
MICHAEL YOUNG

PREVIOUS PAGES Residents of a Ruijin nursing home enjoy a game of gateball, a popular team sport throughout Asia. As with croquet, players must hit a ball through a series of hoops.
LIU SHAONING

RIGHT Seventy-five years later, a handful of Long March veterans are still alive, including 98-year-old Liu Jiaqi. Born in September 1913 in Ruijin, Liu joined the Red Army in 1929, and set off on the Long March in 1934. He was injured at the Battle of Xiang River. Liu, who retired in 1975, is shown here being interviewed in Ruijin by a local television crew.
LIU SHAONING

CHAPTER 10

Pathways to the West

As the Red Army retreated westward from Jiangxi, it struggled with several enemies: Nationalist forces, unforgiving terrain, harsh weather and internal divisions among the Communist leaders. Then in early 1935, a new leadership formed around Mao Zedong, and a new approach to combat, better suited to a peasant uprising, was adopted: guerrilla warfare. The seeds of the eventual success of the Long March had been sown.

The provinces along this section of the Long March—Guangdong, Guangxi, Hunan and Guizhou—have followed distinct paths over the past 75 years.

Interestingly, one of this area's great natural resources, tungsten, played a key role in the early days of the Long March. Chiang Kai-shek had ordered Guangdong warlord Chen Yitang to stop selling the metal to the Jiangxi Soviet's revolutionaries, who needed it to toughen steel in their weapons factories. Annoyed by this loss of revenue, Chen formed a secret alliance with the Red Army. At a critical point, the revolutionaries moved unopposed past the warlord's army and burst through the GMD blockade from Jiangxi into neighbouring Guangxi.

LEFT A simple but sturdy bridge provides a passageway into this Miao village near Liping.

LIU YINGYI

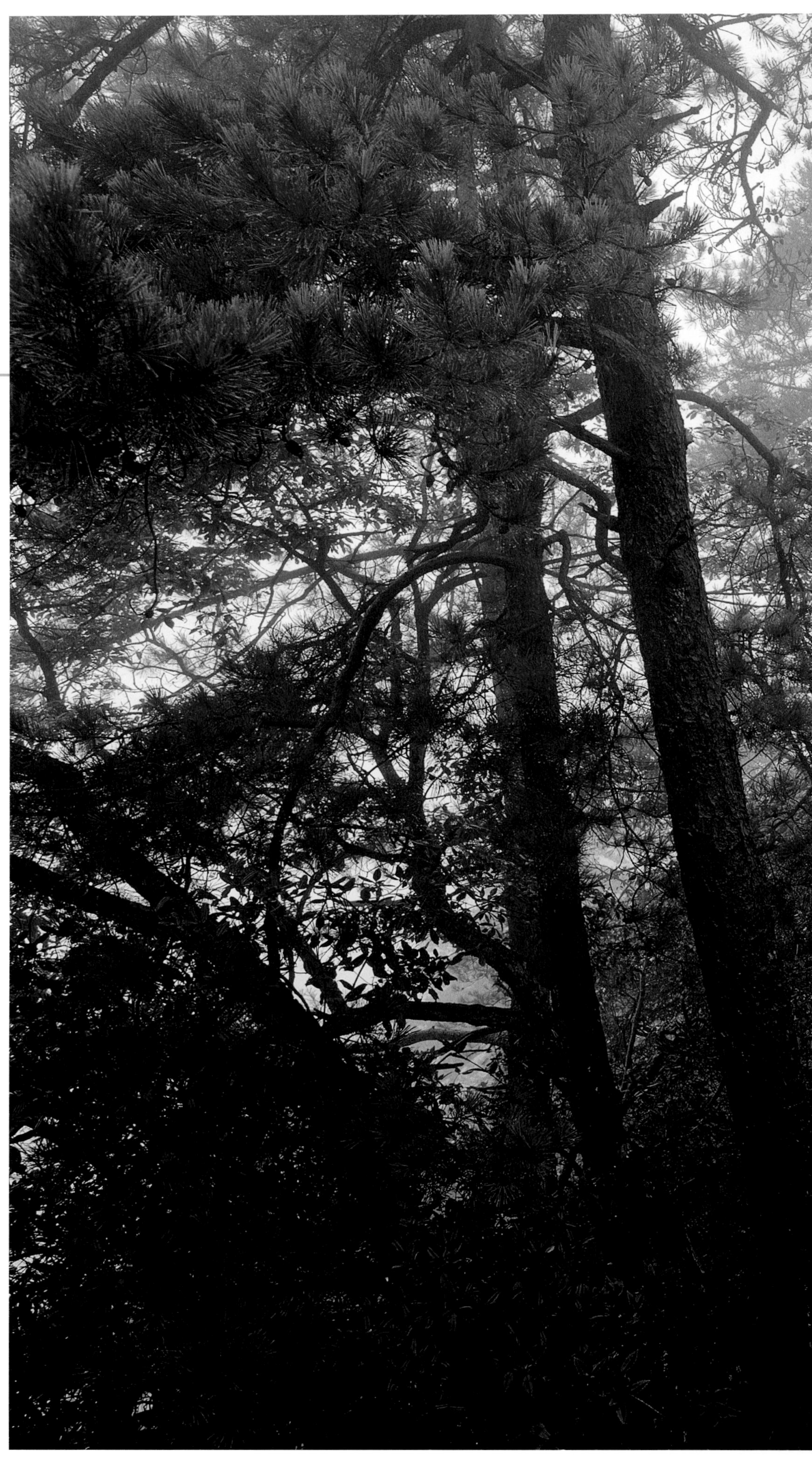

RIGHT The mist-shrouded Zhangjiajie National Forest Park in northern Hunan province is part of the wider Wulingyuan Scenic Area, which is a UNESCO World Heritage Site. In 1982 Zhangjiajie was declared China's first national forest park.
FENG JIANGUO

Today China supplies 85 percent of the world's tungsten, which is mined mostly in Guangdong. The metal is in big demand in jewelry workshops and steel foundries, and tungsten oxides are vital in the manufacture of television monitors, halogen lamps, optical fibers, and ammunition.

But mining is a small part of the picture in this corner of China. Since the early 1980s, Guandong's rice paddies have been transformed into a seemingly endless series of factories—electronics, toys, shoes, textiles—all serviced by a vast network of highways, bridges, railways, power stations and airports. This huge economic powerhouse extends from Shenzen, along the Pearl River and into the neighboring Guangxi Zhuang Autonomous Region.

However, the benefits of development have not always been spread evenly. According to statistics from 2009, Guangxi's per-capita gross domestic product lags well behind that of Guangdong. The Sino-Vietnamese War, which turned much of western Guangxi into a military zone, slowed economic development in the area. Even when the shelling stopped in the late 1980s, minefields remained.

Cross-border trade with Vietnam has picked up during the past two decades, and investors have begun moving industry into Guangxi to

ABOVE A Miao farmer gets a hand from her grandson as she tends her rice crops in Tongdao, Hunan province.
LIU YINGYI

exploit its cheaper labor. And Guangxi is seldom short of tourists: the beautiful landscape along the Li River near Guilin has been an inspiration of poets and painters for centuries.

Guizhou, one of China's poorest provinces, has also struggled. Amid high mountains and deep rivers, just 3 percent of the province's total area is flat land. Floods and droughts are frequent.

Policies initiated under Mao have helped alleviate the situation. The construction of railroads and highways brought Guizhou into the national transport network. And some military industry was moved here in the 1960s and '70s. When Beijing's industrial policies shifted to the production of consumer goods in the 1980s, Guizhou's missile factories began making refrigerators.

Although Guizhou remains poor, provincial authorities are determinedly upbeat. The province's natural reserves of gold, silver, copper, mercury and coal

RIGHT In Zunyi, schoolchildren known as "Wen Ming Tian Shi" (Little Civilized Angels) participate in a program to keep local neighborhoods clean and roads safe. Activities include sweeping streets, picking up litter, helping people at pedestrian crossings and public education.
CATHERINE CROLL

LEFT Customers line up for pearl milk tea, a mixture of tea, fruit, milk and chewy tapioca starch balls, at the Da Si Jiu Pearl Milk Tea shop in the Guilin city prefecture, northern Guangxi province.
LIU YINGYI

have offered development prospects. "As the province attempts to alleviate shortcomings, a high-speed rail line from Guiyang to Guangzhou and other projects meant to expand the province's transportation links with neighboring provinces are in the works, with hopes to spur economic growth," declared a recent Guizhou statement on the economy.

Hunan, Mao's home province, is said to be the site of China's very first farms, and it remains on the cutting edge of agricultural science. Working with a new "super rice" that is resistant to disease and insects and can deliver more grains, the Hunan Agricultural Academy recently produced a world record yield of 12,375 pounds (5,625 kilograms) per acre and plans to increase output a further 60 percent by 2030.

Improving transportation has been a key issue for Hunan. In recent years road construction in the province has outpaced the nation average, and it now boasts 3,700 miles (6,000 kilometers) of expressways. The rough roads joining Changde, site of Hunan's most important industrial development zone, and Jishou, the region's largest city, had changed little in the decades after the Red Army marched through western Hunan. When the US$1.66 billion Changde–Jishou Expressway opened in 2008, travel time between the two cities was cut from 10 hours to four.

Thanks to the commercial opportunities opened up by this gleaming new road, the Changde–Jishou Expressway has been dubbed "Hunan's four-hour economic zone." It is a phenomenon that can been seen throughout this part of China: improved transportation links, growing investment and a lively entrepreneurial spirit have helped create a massive economic zone that is accelerating into the 21st century.

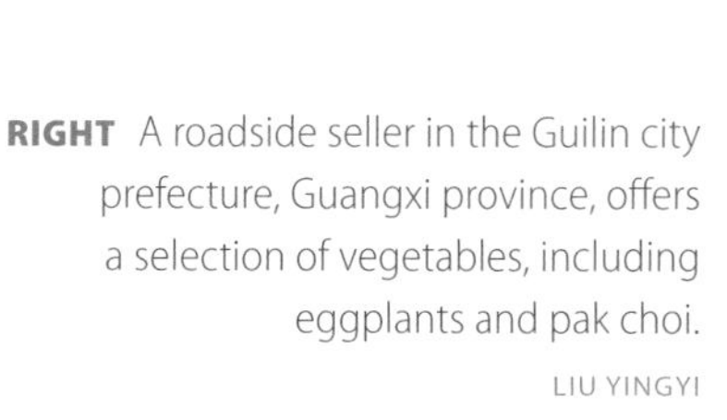

RIGHT A roadside seller in the Guilin city prefecture, Guangxi province, offers a selection of vegetables, including eggplants and pak choi.
LIU YINGYI

Guizhou has significant numbers of Yao, Miao, Yi, Qiang, Dong, Zhuang, Buyi, Bai, Tujia, Gelao and Shui people, making it one of China's most ethnically diverse provinces. In total, minority groups account for nearly 40 percent of the province's population.

FOLLOWING PAGES Reflecting growing environmental awareness in China, these girls have donned green ribbons and formed the "Children's Green Volunteer Group" in Guiyang, Guizhou province. Their main activity is picking up litter in the streets and lanes around their homes. The local shopkeepers thank each of the girls as they clean up the sidewalks and gutters outside their businesses.
CATHERINE CROLL

Lucky
08

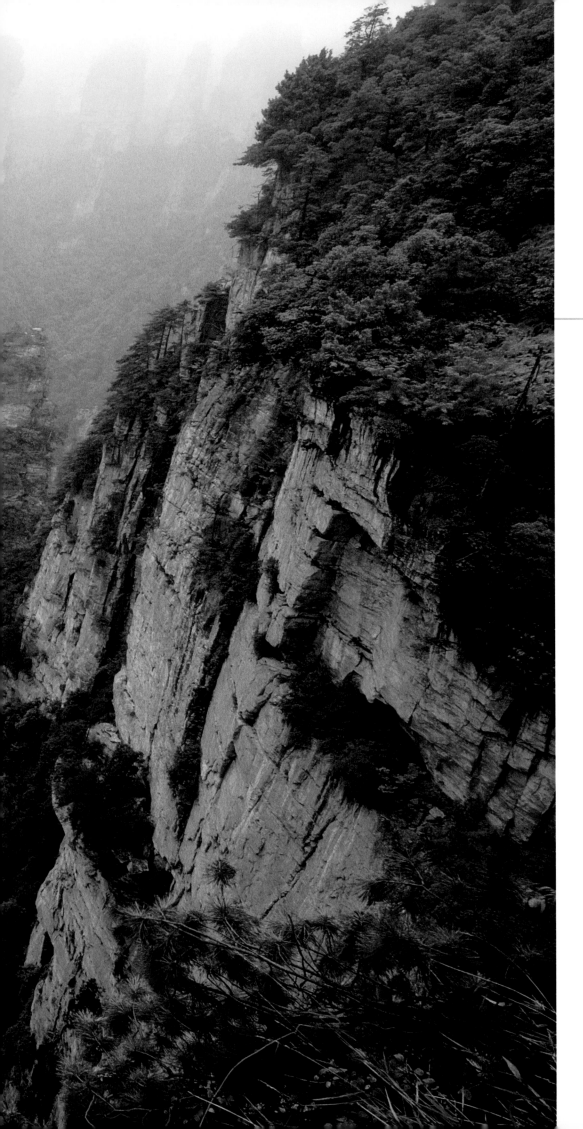

LEFT The quartz and sandstone pillars in Zhangjiajie National Forest Park, created by thousands of years of erosion, are believed to be the inspiration for the floating Hallelujah Mountains on the planet Pandora in the hit movie *Avatar*. In fact, one of the pillars was renamed Avatar Hallelujah Mountain in 2010.
FENG JIANGUO

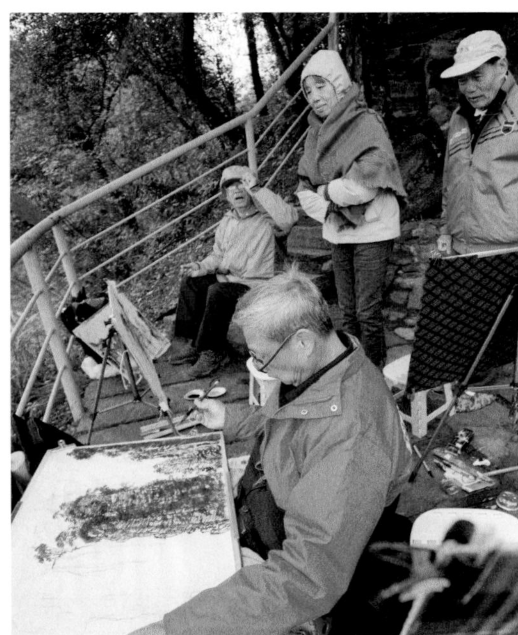

ABOVE The distinctive stone formations of Zhangjiajie National Forest Park can be found in many ancient Chinese paintings. Here a group of artists continues the tradition by sketching one of the park's 3,000 pillars.
FENG JIANGUO

FOLLOWING PAGES A Muslim street seller offers lamb shashlik in the old town of Phoenix City, Hunan province. The city, which has an exceptionally well-preserved old quarter, has a large number of the Miao and Tujia minorities. It was the center of the Miao Rebellion of 1854–73, which prompted a brutal crackdown by China's Qing rulers. Following the rebellion, many of the surviving Miao people fled China.
FENG JIANGUO

隆源山寨
苗家小吃
苗家香豆腐
铁板香土豆
苗家臭豆腐
1314160453
隆源
苗家
冰酸梅汤

苗家
冰凉粉
桃
湘
提供导游
环保

PREVIOUS PAGES A villager dries corn in the village of Tunbao in the Anshun area of Guizhou province. Ethnologists refer to villagers in the Anshun area as "Tunbao" people, encompassing both the military ("tun") and commercial ("bao") history of these villages.
HEI MING

BELOW General He Long Red Army School in Sangzhi county, Hunan province, stands in memory of the commander of the Second Front Army. He, who was born in Sangzhi, launched the Second Front Army's leg of the Long March from this area.
FENG JIANGUO

RIGHT Slippers left outside to dry provide a colorful contrast to this weather-worn house in Longsheng, Guangxi province.

LIU YINGYI

15807406937
发艺

ABOVE A tobacco salesman works on the streets of Tong Ren, Guizhou province. With a history of growing tobacco that dates back more than 250 years, Tong Ren is China's third largest producer of tobacco.
FENG JIANGUO

PREVIOUS PAGES A lime and mandarin seller plies his trade in Yuan Ling, Hunan province. Hunan is one of China's major citrus-growing areas.
FENG JIANGUO

RIGHT This row of shops is in the town of Liping, Guizhou province. Large parts of Guizhou are designated as autonomous regions for the province's many minority groups. Liping is mostly populated by the southern Dong people, perhaps best known for their carpentry skills and singing.
LIU YINGYI

LEFT A group of men gather for a match of Xiangqi in the town of Liping. Also known as Chinese chess, Xiangqi is a popular board game in China and among Chinese communities around the world. As with chess, two players line up their pieces on opposite sides of a board. The goal is to capture the opposing player's "general."

LIU YINGYI

BELOW This church in Yuan Ling county, Hunan province, was built in 1904. Although it was initially a Catholic church, since 1950 it has been run by a Chinese Christian committee for western Hunan, which now has 485 members.

FENG JIANGUO

FOLLOWING PAGES Longsheng villager Pan Erlin, a member of the Miao minority, still enjoys smoking a pipe at the age of 100 years.

LIU YINGYI

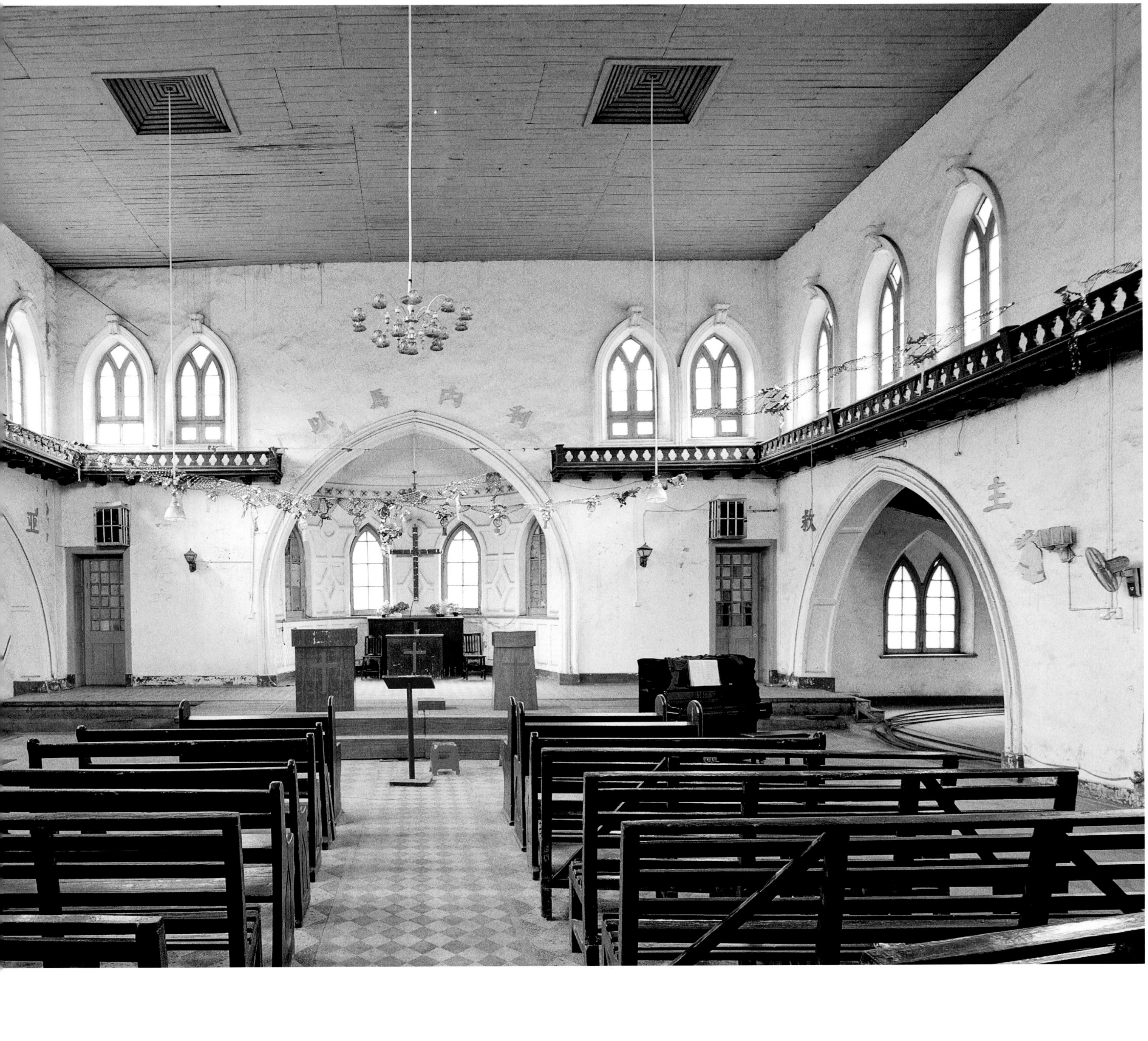

LEFT This family, in Tongdao County, Hunan province, belongs to the Dong ethnic minority. In all, about three million Dong people live in China, mostly in Hunan, Guizhou and Guangxi provinces.
LIU YINGYI

FOLLOWING PAGES The Dragon's Backbone Rice Terraces in Longsheng, Guangxi Zhuang Autonomous Region, date back eight centuries to the time of the Yuan Dynasty. Winding around and up the sides of Longji Mountain, the terraces reach an altitude of 3,600 feet (1,100 meters). They are known as the Dragon's Backbone because the terraces are said to resemble a dragon's scales, while the ridge at the summit looks like its backbone.
LIU YINGYI

RIGHT A Miao family in Longsheng prepares food in a large pot over an open fire. Most Miao families eat sour soup, which is made by fermenting rice or tofu water in a large pot for three to five days. Sour soup often includes meat, fish or a variety of vegetables, which is salted to help preserve it as the soup is prepared.

LIU YINGYI

FOLLOWING PAGES The rice is almost ready for harvesting on this farm near Xingyi, Guizhou province.

HEI MING

PREVIOUS PAGES Bing'an Ancient Town on the Chishui River was an important gateway to Guizhou from south Sichuan during the Ming and Qing Dynasties. Because of its isolated position, many of Bing'an's historic buildings have survived, though the town does have some modern structures, including a new bridge.
CATHERINE CROLL

ABOVE In early 1935, Red Army troops clashed with Nationalist forces near the Tucheng old town on the Chishui River.
CATHERINE CROLL

RIGHT Laborers in Tucheng old town, who make their living hauling gravel, take a well-earned rest.
CATHERINE CROLL

泥水工
维修;装修
电话,15120118742

PREVIOUS PAGES This apartment building on the northern outskirts of Guiyang city is typical of new residential developments in China, with apartments on the upper floors and space for retail and commercial operators facing the street on the ground level.
CATHERINE CROLL

BELOW An elevated roadway cuts through the countryside near Xingyi. A growing number of freeways in the region use this style of construction to minimize the impact on farming land and to overcome the constantly rising and falling terrain.
HEI MING

RIGHT Nong Min has worked in the fields near the village of Chang Gang, Guizhou province, for eight decades. Although she is now in her 90s, she must continue working because she has outlived her husband and both of her sons.
CATHERINE CROLL

LEFT These boys in the village of Ban Qiao, Guizhou province, sport distinctive traditional haircuts. The practice of shaving the heads of young boys on the sides and back and leaving a long patch in the front is believed either to ward off evil spirits or to help balance the natural energies of Earth, Fire, Air and Water.
CATHERINE CROLL

FOLLOWING PAGES This late-night food stall in Zunyi, Guizhou province, offers "New Orleans Grilled Chicken Wings." The sign behind the stall marks the entrance to an "Internet bar."
CATHERINE CROLL

明珠
网吧

新奥尔良烤翅
电话:15121208105
回味无穷。

简介
遵义红色印象为了纪
念伟大领袖毛主席而筹建
的场厅
红色印象所在的位置
是当年著名的红军街，位
于遵义会议会址正对面，
遵义人民对红军有深厚的
感情，在遵义有红军山，
有红军菩萨，“红军菩
萨”救穷人，“红军菩萨
显圣”还有关于红军种种
神话传说色彩
1935年1月召开的遵义
的领导地位，在极其危急的
拯救了中国革命，是党历史
会议决定了红军的命运，中
中国共产党的生驱者的命运
转运，红色印象陈列的怀念
遵义转运的灵气，并特设
位游客能在遵义接纳点

LEFT Lou Mingxian was 11 years old when the Red Army passed through his hometown of Tucheng. He recalls that the officers slept in the houses and thousands of soldiers slept in the narrow cobbled streets. All of the wooden front doors in the town were used to build a bridge so the army could cross the Chishui River. Lou's two older brothers joined the Red Army when it left, and the family never heard from them again.

CATHERINE CROLL

ABOVE Zunyi played a crucial role in the history of modern China, with Mao Zedong securing his position as leader of the Communist Party during the Zunyi Conference in 1935. Today local merchants adorn their shops with Mao memorabilia. This business even offers tourists a chance to have their picture taken "with Chairman Mao"—with a little help from Photoshop.
CATHERINE CROLL

RIGHT Two young friends in the village of Banqiaozhen, Guizhou province.
CATHERINE CROLL

PREVIOUS PAGES Miao Red Village in Xingyi City is nestled next to farmland in Guizhou province.

HEI MING

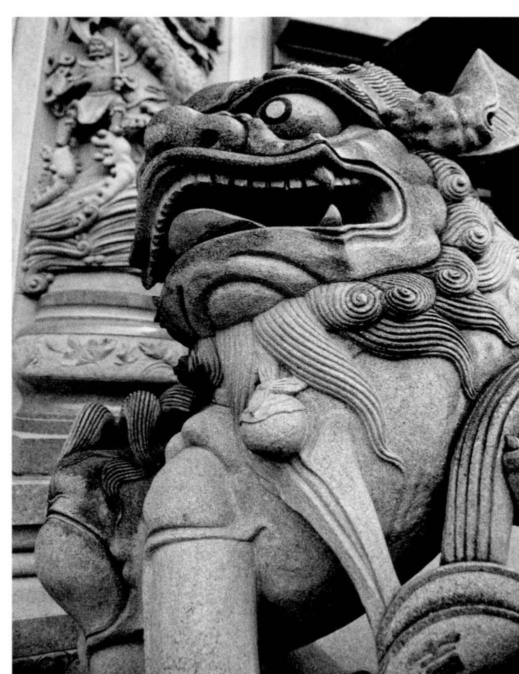

ABOVE This lion adorns the main Buddhist temple in Zunyi. In Buddhism, the lion represents both the Buddha himself, who according to some accounts was the son of a king, and his teachings, which are sometimes called "the lion's roar."

CATHERINE CROLL

LEFT This young girl lives in a warren of tiny houses nestled between the Tucheng old town and the Chishui River. The outer walls of the houses have been used by children to draw pictures and practice writing.

CATHERINE CROLL

ZOOMLION
ZOOMLION

中国驰名商标
展示柜
雪花

PREVIOUS PAGES Support columns for a high-speed rail line rise up from the hills along the Chishui River in the Tucheng area of Guizhou province. China is undergoing a massive expansion of its rail network, with eight major new rail corridors and over 15,000 miles (25,000 kilometers) of new rail lines planned by 2020.

CATHERINE CROLL

LEFT Two Yi minority children oversee a roadside stall selling drinks in Xundian, Yunnan province. Stalls are common in this area, serving the constant stream of trucks traveling between Guizhou and Yunnan provinces.

HEI MING

FOLLOWING PAGES Memorials to the Long March can be found all along its route. In Xingyi City, Guizhou province, local children stand beneath a poster depicting the reunion of the First Front Army and the Fourth Front Army, marking the end of the Long March.

HEI MING

Paris

一九三五年十月十三日，中共中央率领
陕甘支队胜利到达陕北吴起镇，宣告了历
时一年，纵横11省，长驱二万五千里的长
征胜利结束。

大海粮油工业(防城港)有

CHAPTER 11

The Sichuan Powerhouse and Beyond

As he sought food and rural recruits for the retreating Red Army in 1934, Mao Zedong chose lush Sichuan province as their initial destination. But by the time the First Front Army had begun the long trek northward through Sichuan, the main goal was simply one of staying alive. Across the varied landscapes of the Dadu River valley, the soaring Great Snow Mountains and the treacherous Great Grasslands, thousands of Red Army soldiers succumbed to the murderous conditions or died in battle. Those who survived embodied the unbreakable spirit of the Long March.

Today, that unmistakable spirit can be found throughout Sichuan and Yunnan provinces—in the history and culture, food, natural wealth, industry, and the genius and energy of the people. The region's central secret is an abundance of water. Indeed, the name Sichuan derives from the phrase "Four Circuits of Rivers and Gorges."

LEFT Farm laborers near Xichang, Sichuan province, work on the rice harvest. They are placing the freshly harvested rice into a machine that separates the grains of rice from the rest of the plant.
WANG WENLAN

RIGHT A group of children at a school near the village of Butou, Sichuan province, give the Young Pioneers salute. The Young Pioneers of China, which is run by the Communist Youth League, has an estimated 130 million members. The maps in the background proclaim the Chinese saying: "Look out for the motherland but be aware of the world."
WANG WENLAN

The largest of these rivers, the Yangzi, sweeps rich topsoil from as far away as the Himalayas into the fertile Red Basin. Here, some 16 million acres (6.5 million hectares) of farmland provide food for the area's 80 million people. In all, Sichuan produces 10 percent of China's pork, 8 percent of its cooking oil, and 6 percent of its rice, wheat and other grain.

The region's rivers are also central to China's massive hydroelectric power program. Although China's most ambitious project, the Three Gorges Dam, is located to the east in Hubei province, Sichuan has its share of major hydroelectric installations, notably on the Dadu, Jinsha and Yalong rivers in the southwest of the province. By 2015, Sichuan is forecast to generate 30 gigawatts of power.

The Great Grasslands of the Rou'ergai Plateau, where the Red Army suffered so much, are part of China's 23,000 square miles (60,000 square kilometers) of mountain wetlands. Most of them are peat lands up to 10 yards (10 meters) thick. The peat layers, which function like a sponge making them more than 90 percent water, are major reservoirs that help maintain water levels in streams and rivers to the east.

A US$3.2 million United Nations-sponsored program in the grasslands region is preserving lands affected

世界政区
放眼世界
面向世界
面向未来

by unsustainable farming practices, mining, infrastructure development and climate change.

The emergence of Sichuan's industrial economy may be traced back to the early 1960s, when Beijing declared that the country needed to prepare for a major war. "Dig tunnels deep; store grain everywhere," Chairman Mao instructed. Sichuan was designated as part of the "third front." The expected war never happened, but the factories remained and diversified beyond defense manufacturing. Today the region is China's biggest producer of motorcycles, and a leader in steel, aluminum, automotive and chemical production.

The area is also rich in history. Some 3,000 years ago, two rival kingdoms, Ba and Shu, established themselves here. The first known use of firearms was recorded during the six-year-long Battle of Xiangyang in the 13th century. And after Japanese forces sacked Chiang Kai-shek's capital Nanjing in 1937, the Generalissimo moved his headquarters to Chongqing.

These days traces of this recent history make the area a popular tourist destination for increasingly affluent Chinese. In Chongqing, tourist hordes visit such landmarks as Zhou Enlai's office, a museum celebrating the exploits of the Eighth Route Army, which was formed from Red Army units that fought alongside the Nationalists against the Japanese. Scores of tunnels that served as air-raid shelters during the Sino-Japanese War now house small businesses near central Chongqing.

The region's economic growth is no more evident than in Chongqing, today a mega-city of well over 30 million people. To better manage the city's booming economy, which is expanding at a steady 8 to 9 percent annually, Beijing

ABOVE China's many large-scale infrastructure projects include this freeway, bridge and tunnel along the Dadu River valley in central Sichuan province.

MICHAEL YOUNG

RIGHT Goats feed precariously above a sheer drop of over 1,000 feet (300 meters) next to the main road linking the towns of Lijian and Shangri-la, Yunnan province.

SEBASTIEN MICKE

ABOVE Tibetan students are studying hard at a primary school near the town of Danba. This area sits inside the Ganzi Tibetan Autonomous Prefecture, whose population is roughly four-fifths Tibetan.
LI FAN

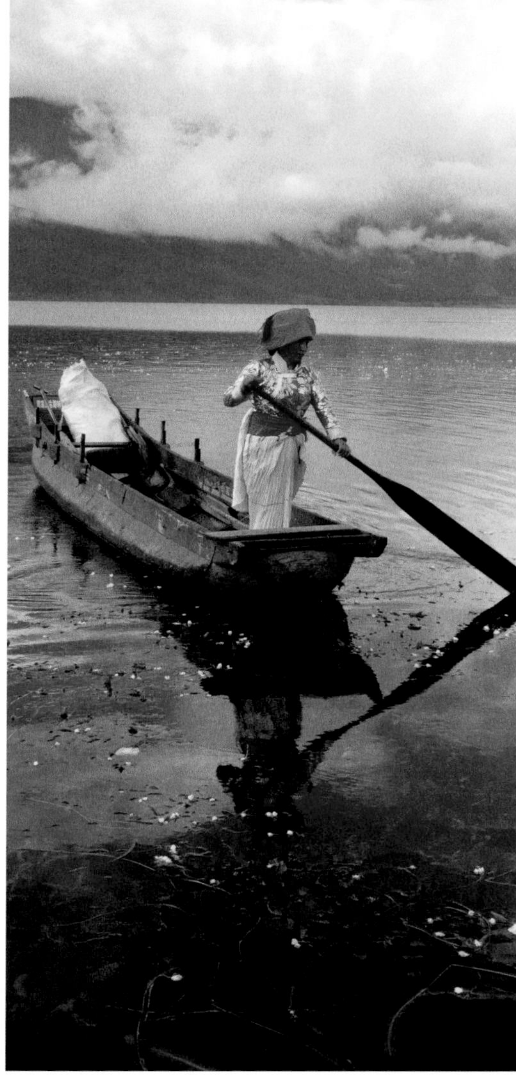

RIGHT A woman paddles across Lugu Lake, north of Xichang. According to legend, this area has the most beautiful women in Sichuan.
WANG WENLAN

FAR RIGHT Corn dries in the sun in the town of Mianning, north of Lugu Lake. Dried corn is a main ingredient in corn bread, corn flour and the grain alcohol Baijou, which is also known as firewater.
WANG WENLAN

in 1997 designated Chongqing as a distinct administrative area that deals directly with the central government.

The city's soaring ambition appears infectious. On Chongqing's outskirts small townships have begun widening their main streets. "Every town around here thinks that it will one day be as big as New York City," says Ding Lintong, who runs a number of Sichuan businesses.

Vast development in China's southwest has had a price, with dirty air and water threatening the quality of life in the region's urban areas. Clean-up efforts

are now a priority. The Chongqing government is developing a cap-and-trade scheme to get factories to cut energy use, has slashed land costs for green-friendly businesses, and has sponsored tree planting.

Local businesses are following suit. Tailu Puji is manufacturing products that cut oil use in vehicles, ships and power plants, and Chang'an, the nation's fourth-largest automaker, is manufacturing zero-emission electric vehicles.

Despite the enormity of China's ecological problems, optimism prevails. "If Chongqing can succeed in transforming into a green, low-carbon city, there's no doubt that the rest of Chinese cities will be able to make this switch," economist Li Yong of the Chongqing Academy of Social Sciences told the *New York Times*.

Although Yunnan sits far from the centers of political and economic power, it has played a significant role in China's dealings with the outside world. It was where China's borders touched on French interests (the Indochina colonies) and the British Empire (Burma and India). Today those neighboring territories are very much in charge of their own affairs: Cambodia, Laos, Malaysia, Myanmar (Burma), Thailand and Vietnam.

Connecting the southwest to the world was nevertheless a slow process. Not until the early 1990s were its borders opened to trade with Myanmar, Laos and Vietnam, and not until almost 2000 was the national rail network extended to west Yunnan. But over the past decade the province's ties with Asia and the world have expanded dramatically. Yunnan now has nine entry points for visitors from Vietnam, Myanmar and Laos. In the year ending June 2011, a total of 1.79 million people joined

RIGHT These members of the Naxi ethnic minority are gathered in the old town of Lijiang, Yunnan province. In much of China, children are cared for, and even raised, by grandparents while their parents work in the cities, in the countryside or as migrant workers.
SEBASTIEN MICKE

one-day inbound trips to Yunnan from these countries, an increase of almost 25 percent over the previous year.

As elsewhere, transportation is playing a central role in the province's development. The 1100-mile (1800-kilometer) Kunming–Bangkok highway, the first international expressway out of China, opened in 2008, cutting the driving time to the Thai capital in half to 20 hours. And in 2020, the 2,400-mile (3,900-kilometer) Kunming–Singapore High-Speed Railway will open Yunnan to the 300 million people living in the Mekong River Basin.

For evidence of Yunnan's growing role in the world, look no further than the mammoth Luosiwan International Trade Centre in downtown Kunming. China's largest distribution hub for small commodities, the market attracts 300,000 visitors a day, nearly one-third of them international buyers in search of toys, clothing, plastic goods and ornaments.

The Yunnanese used to celebrate their isolation with the proverb: "The mountains are high and the emperor is far away." The mountains in the southwest are still high, but the rest of the world is getting much closer, to everyone's benefit.

PREVIOUS PAGES A man in the old town of Lijiang draws the attention of a couple of spectators.
SEBASTIEN MICKE

RIGHT This elevated highway crosses a section of the Min River that was flooded following the construction of dams downriver. This area northwest of Chengdu, known as Wenchuan, is near to the epicenter of the 2008 earthquakes that killed 68,000 people.
LI FAN

ABOVE AND RIGHT A group of men gather in Lijiang old town to play mahjongg. The game, which originated in China, is normally played by four people. One myth suggests that Confucius, the Chinese philosopher, developed mahjongg sometime around 500 BC.
SEBASTIEN MICKE

FOLLOWING PAGES A family from the Yi minority heads to market along a mountain road in Butuo county, Sichuan province.
WANG WENLAN

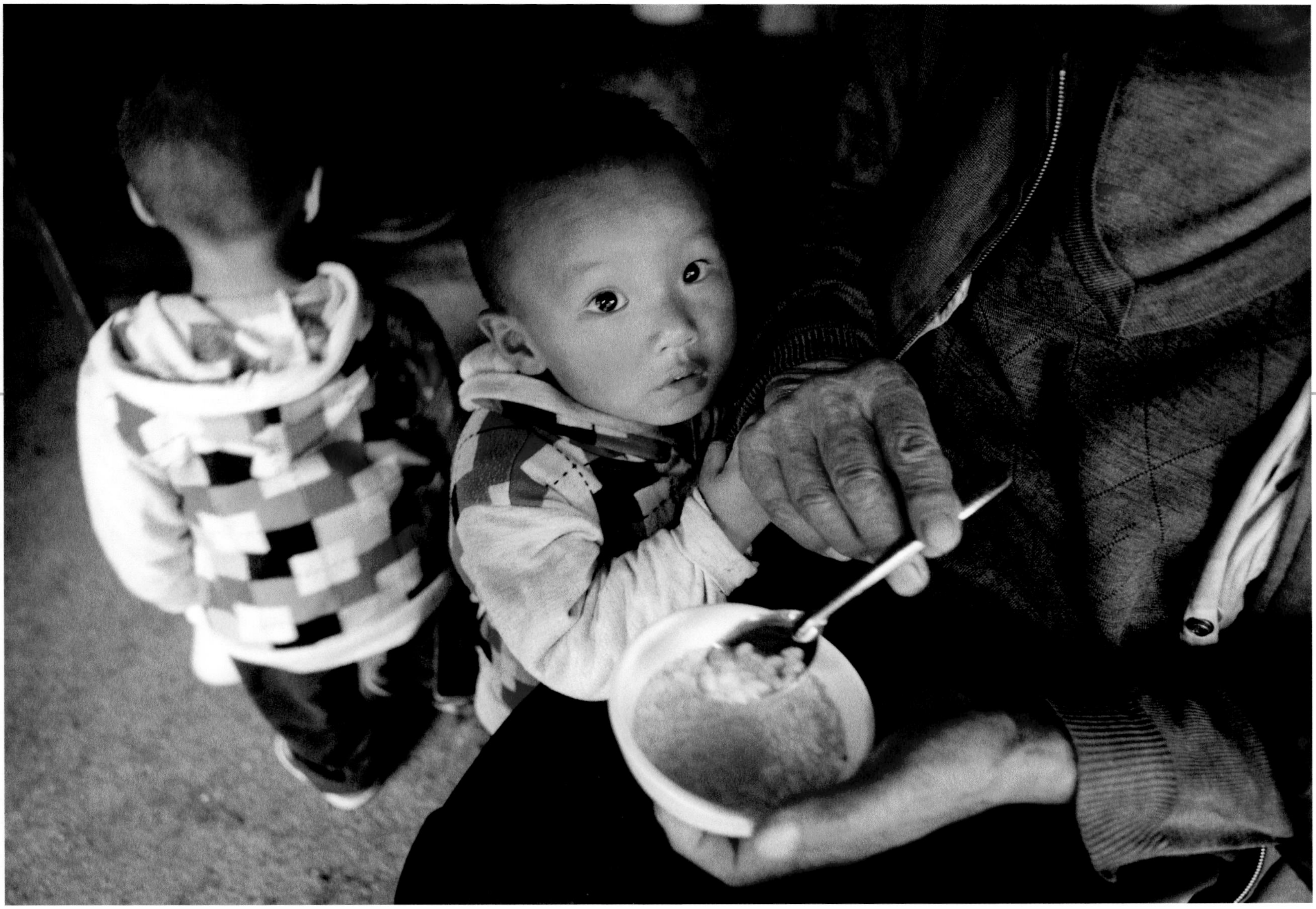

ABOVE An ethnic Naxi child enjoys a bowl of rice congee. Although it has many variations, congee is most often prepared by cooking rice in water for a prolonged period, causing it to break down into a soupy liquid.
SEBASTIEN MICKE

LEFT A yak adorned with colorful ribbons stands ready to take tourists for joyrides around Lijiang old town. Yaks are a common sight throughout the Tibetan Plateau. Domesticated yaks are an important source of milk, meat and fur in this area, and are used as pack animals.
SEBASTIEN MICKE

FAR LEFT This woman in Lijiang belongs to the Yi minority. During the Long March, the Yi set aside their hostility toward outsiders and helped the Red Army as it moved through western China.
SEBASTIEN MICKE

PREVIOUS PAGES Villagers in the Lugu Lake area collect sunflower seeds and hang chilis to dry.

WANG WENLAN

LEFT A Naxi man shows off a prized bird in Lijiang old town, where traders gather to buy and sell birds of prey, including eagles, falcons and goshawks. The birds are used to hunt pheasants and other animals. This traditional form of hunting is believed to date back to the 13th century, when soldiers in Kublai Khan's army taught falconry to the local people.

SEBASTIEN MICKE

FOLLOWING PAGES This hilltop temple is located on the outskirts of Lijiang. Numerous temples, mostly connected to the Naxi faith, can be found in the hills of this area.

SEBASTIEN MICKE

LEFT A villager on the outskirts of Butou collects cornstalks and leaves to make a fire for cooking.

WANG WENLAN

BELOW Legs and sides of lamb have been hung out for sale in Xinjiang old town, Sichuan province.

WANG WENLAN

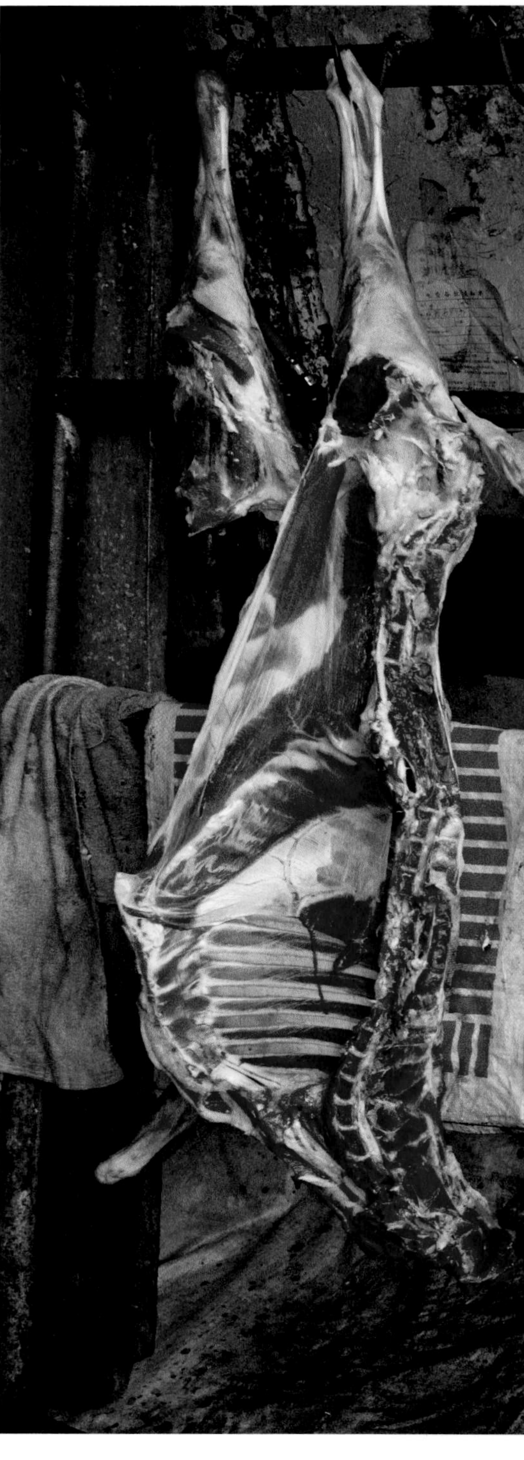

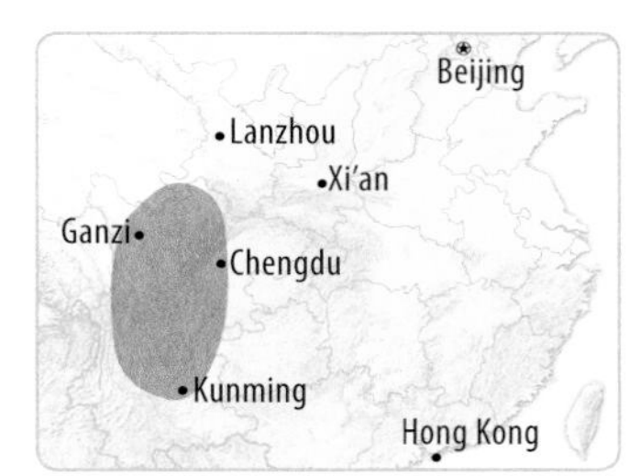

PREVIOUS PAGES Ethnic Naxi villagers in Butou collect plants to be used as feed for their cattle.
WANG WENLAN

FOLLOWING PAGES A Red Army veteran relaxes at his home near the town of Kangding, Sichuan province.
LI FAN

LEFT This young woman from the Lugu Lake area is a member of the Naxi minority.
WANG WENLAN

PREVIOUS PAGES Striking limestone terraces sit among the rugged valleys of Baishuitai, Yunnan province.
SEBASTIEN MICKE

ABOVE These primary schoolchildren attend a Hope School near Xichang, Sichuan province. Thousands of Hope Schools, which are set up in poorer areas of China, are funded by Project Hope using donations collected from across the country.

WANG WENLAN

RIGHT Horses used to give tourists rides around the Lugu Lake area are adorned with colorful saddles and blankets.

WANG WENLAN

LEFT Pig-trough boats, known as *zhucaochuan* in the local language, are a common sight on Lugu Lake. Straddling the border of Yunnan and Sichuan provinces, Lugu Lake sits at an elevation of 8,900 feet (2,690 meters).
WANG WENLAN

Beijing
Lanzhou
Xi'an
Ganzi
Chengdu
Kunming
Hong Kong

LEFT Autumn brings a wide array of flowers into bloom around Lugu Lake.

WANG WENLAN

BELOW A herbal medicine seller lays out a huge selection of products in Xichang old town. The sign on the wall proclaims: "High level professional herbal medicine can save people's lives!"

WANG WENLAN

FOLLOWING PAGES The Lugu area is home to members of the Tibetan, Yi, Pumi and Norzu ethnic minorities, as well as the Mosuo people, one of the few societies in the world in which the family name passes from the mother rather than the father.

WANG WENLAN

川凉泸沽湖116号准载7人
泸沽湖026号准载7人

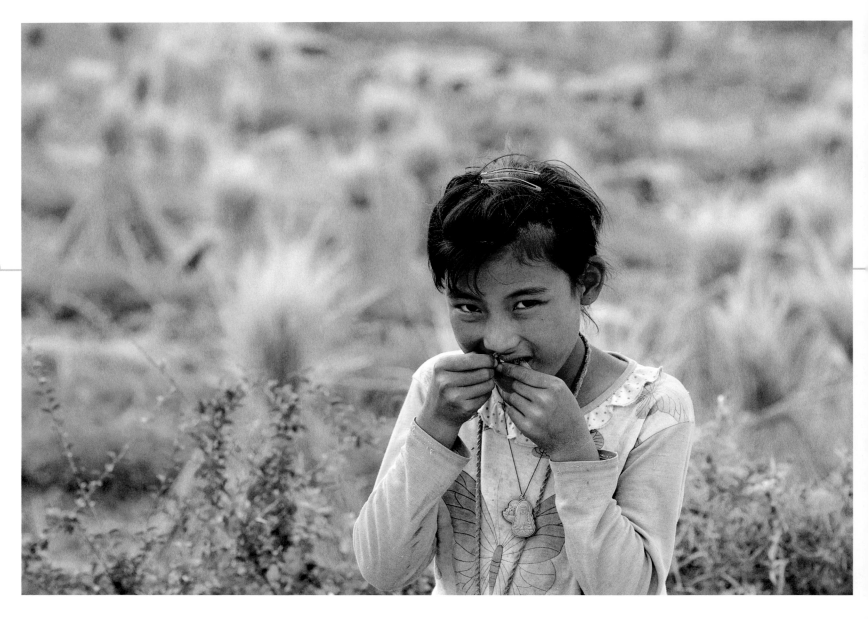

ABOVE A girl helps herself to some sunflower seeds in Da Miao Cun (Big Miao Village) near Xichang.
WANG WENLAN

RIGHT These brightly embroidered insoles are for sale in Da Miao Cun.
WANG WENLAN

FAR RIGHT This elderly Miao woman lives in Da Miao Cun. The Miao, whose presence in China dates as far back as 5,000 BC, tended to settle in hilly regions that could be cultivated. Although they were once known for growing opium, today they cultivate more socially acceptable crops like potatoes, soybeans, sugarcane, peanuts and cotton.
WANG WENLAN

PREVIOUS PAGES Apple harvest time in the village of Yan Yuan, Sichuan province.
WANG WENLAN

LEFT The Bridge of Iron Chains, scene of one of the most celebrated battles of the Long March, still spans the Dadu River in the town of Luding, Sichuan province. Local residents continue to use it as a footbridge, but most traffic in the area crosses the modern bridges found downstream.
LIANG DAMING

泸定县支公司
指定医疗机构
泸定县人民医院
二级乙等医院
定点机构
甘孜州爱卫会

LEFT The windows of a modern hospital in Luding reflect the change that is happening all along the Long March route as old buildings make way for new.
LIANG DAMING

BELOW A young girl watches the exercises that take place every evening in Luding's main square. The exercises include a series of dance routines performed by ordinary citizens.
LIANG DAMING

ABOVE A young boy minds his parents' grain store at the central markets in Luding.
LIANG DAMING

RIGHT The central produce market in Luding offers a huge variety of fruits and vegetables.
LIANG DAMING

62
61

LEFT The Dadu River has numerous reservoirs created by hydroelectric dams. In all, the Dadu and its tributaries account for nearly one-quarter of all the hydroelectric power generated in Sichuan province.

MICHAEL YOUNG

FOLLOWING PAGES This is a typical stone blockhouse of the Jiarong Tibetans in Xinduqiao, Ganzi Tibetan Autonomous Prefecture. The fort-like dwellings are usually two or three stories high, with the kitchen and a livestock area on the ground floor, living space on the middle floor, and a shrine and a loft to store drying grain at the top.

SHI YONGTING

ABOVE A Tibetan mother supervises her daughter's studies at their home near Xiaojin, Sichuan province.
RICHARD MCLAREN

LEFT Colorful window decorations brighten up the gray stones of the Jiarong style of Tibetan architecture.
SHI YONGTING

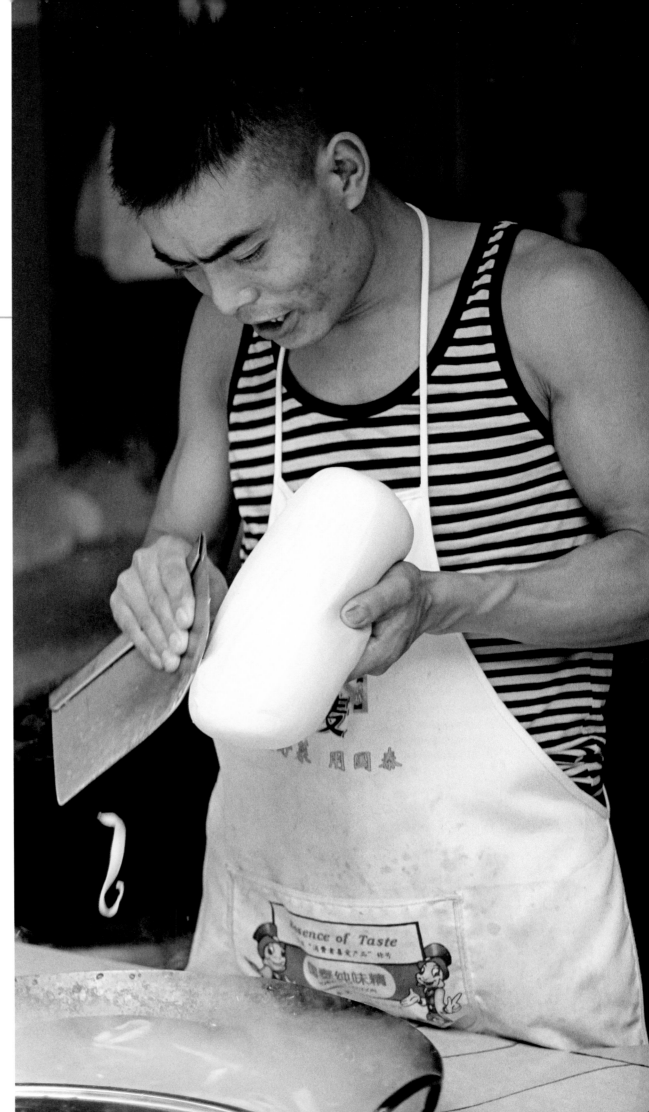

RIGHT A Han Chinese chef prepares *dao xiao mian*, also known as knife slice noodles, in Luding. The act of slicing noodles directly into the pan requires a precise cutting action. In this photo, a noodle can be seen falling midair.

MICHAEL YOUNG

PREVIOUS PAGES Mist rises up between the mountains outside of Kangding in western Sichuan province.

SHI YONGTING

LEFT The remains of a chain bridge stretch across a tributary of the Dadu River north of Xiaojin.

SHI YONGTING

BELOW A local family heads to town in Xiaojin county. The forest beside them is stunted because this area is more than 10,000 feet (3,000 meters) above sea level.

SHI YONGTING

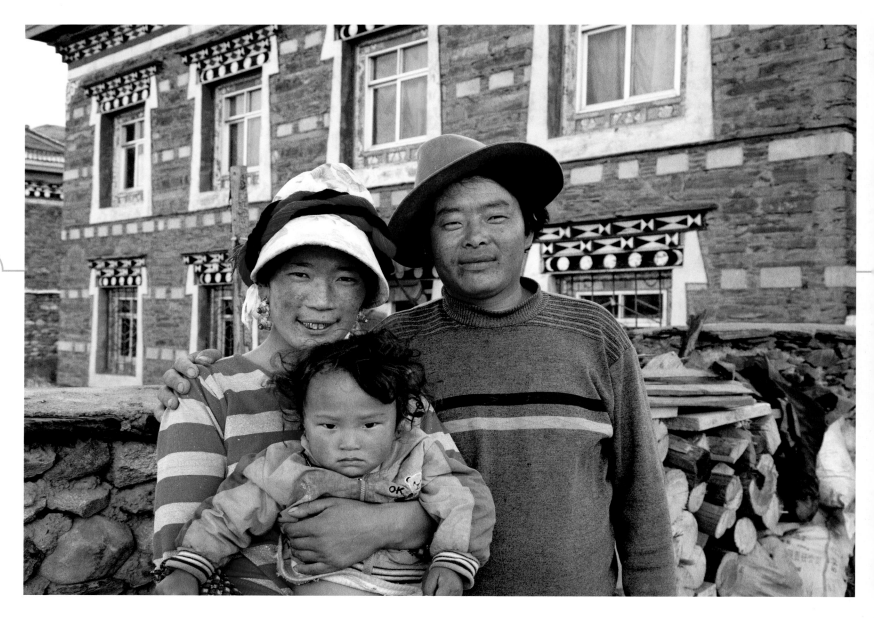

ABOVE This family of Jiarong Tibetans lives near Kangding.
SHI YONGTING

RIGHT This Tibetan Buddhist holy space was created in a structure resembling a tent in Gaisang village, Tagong area, in western Sichuan. The colors of the fabric and prayer flags have specific meanings—blue represents the sky, white for the clouds, red for fire and yellow for the earth.
SHI YONGTING

FAR RIGHT A village girl north of Luding enjoys the area's bountiful supply of water.
MICHAEL YOUNG

LEFT A Tibetan woman in Danba county, Sichuan province, holds beads used during meditation.

LI FAN

PREVIOUS PAGES Siguniangshan National Park, Sichuan province, is perhaps best known for the Four Maidens Mountains. According to Tibetan legend, four sisters were reincarnated as the peaks, which range in height from 17,700 to 20,600 feet (5,355 to 6,250 meters).

SHI YONGTING

ABOVE A street food seller in the town of Maerkang, Sichuan province, prepares Sichuan-style dumplings with shallots, herbs, chili and pork.
RICHARD MCLAREN

RIGHT A woman carries a bunch of pak choi cabbage in Maerkang.
RICHARD MCLAREN

PREVIOUS PAGES This extended family lives in a tent made of woven yak hair in Danba county, Sichuan province.

LI FAN

LEFT Every year from October 1 to January 15, Tibetan Buddhists gather at Tagong Temple in Kangding, Sichuan province, for the Grand Peace Dharma Assembly. During the assembly, as many as 100,000 people chant sutras and pray for world peace and prosperity.

LI FAN

BELOW A boy paints a Tibetan script on a rock in the town of Tagong. The script, "Om Name Padme Om," is a Buddhist mantra associated with the four-armed Shadakshari form of Avalokiteshvara, the bodhisattva of compassion.

LI FAN

ABOVE Locals gather around the prayer wheels at a Buddhist temple in the town of Tagong. According to the Tibetan Buddhist tradition, spinning prayer wheels has much the same meritorious effect as reciting prayers.

LI FAN

RIGHT AND FAR RIGHT For the Grand Peace Dharma Assembly, the grounds of the Tagong Temple are decorated with prayer flags as far as the eye can see, including hundreds hung from a pole rising some 40 feet (13 meters) into the air.

LI FAN

ABOVE Two boys run through the village of Danba. The wood piled up on the left is a sign of the long, cold winter to come.
LI FAN

PREVIOUS PAGES In Kangding county, villages were often arranged in defensive positions on the vast mountainsides.
LI FAN

RIGHT A group of Tibetans gathers near Danba for a yak meat barbecue.
LI FAN

PREVIOUS PAGES Longxi in Wenchuan, Sichuan province, is a traditional Qiang village. The Qiang people lived between Tibetans to the north and the Han to the south, and for centuries Wenchuan was a place where these ethnic groups overlapped.

RICHARD MCLAREN

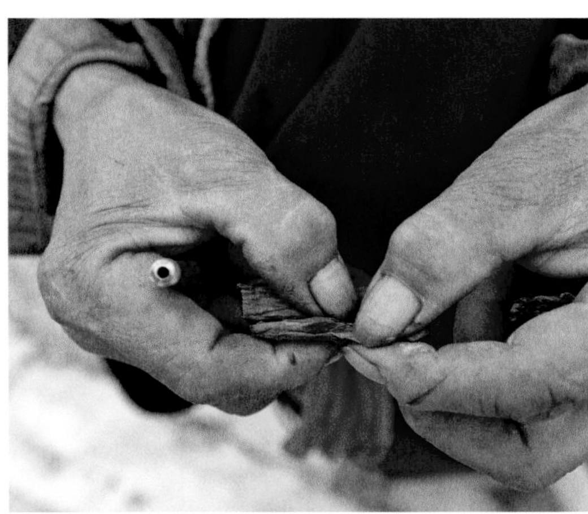

LEFT AND ABOVE An elderly man enjoys his pipe in a Jiarong Tibetan village between Baoxing county and Dawei, Sichuan province. Sichuan is famous for its sun-cured tobacco.

RICHARD MCLAREN

FOLLOWING PAGES The scenic mountains of Danba county provide one of the last remaining refuges for the giant panda.

LI FAN

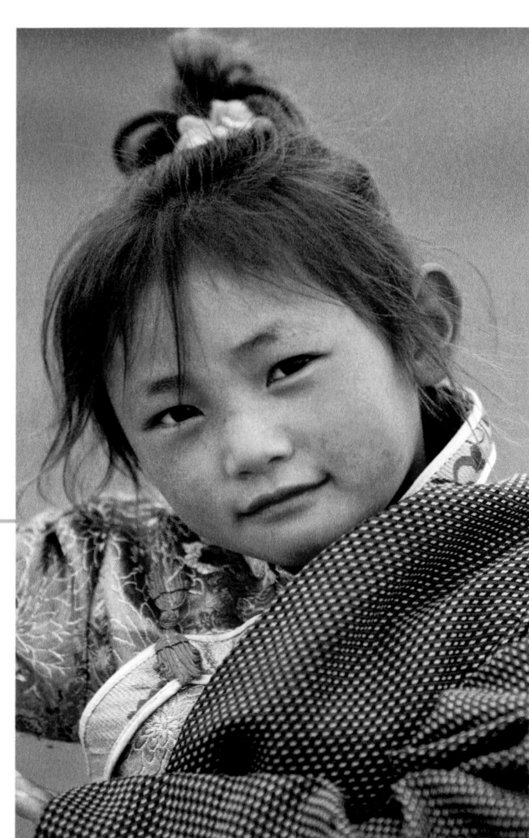

LEFT More than 800,000 Tibetans live in Sichuan province, including this young girl in the town of Hongyuan.
LEO MEIER

ABOVE A Tibetan dragon adorns a building in Zhuokeji, Sichuan province. From designs for painted furniture to elaborate murals in religious buildings, the work of Tibetan artists can be found in virtually every facet of life on the Tibetan plateau.
RICHARD MCLAREN

FOLLOWING PAGES It is easy to imagine that life in the village of Dawei, Sichuan province, has not changed much since the Red Army emerged here after crossing the Great Snow Mountains in June 1935. The last mountain pass that the army came through can be seen on the right.
MICHAEL YOUNG

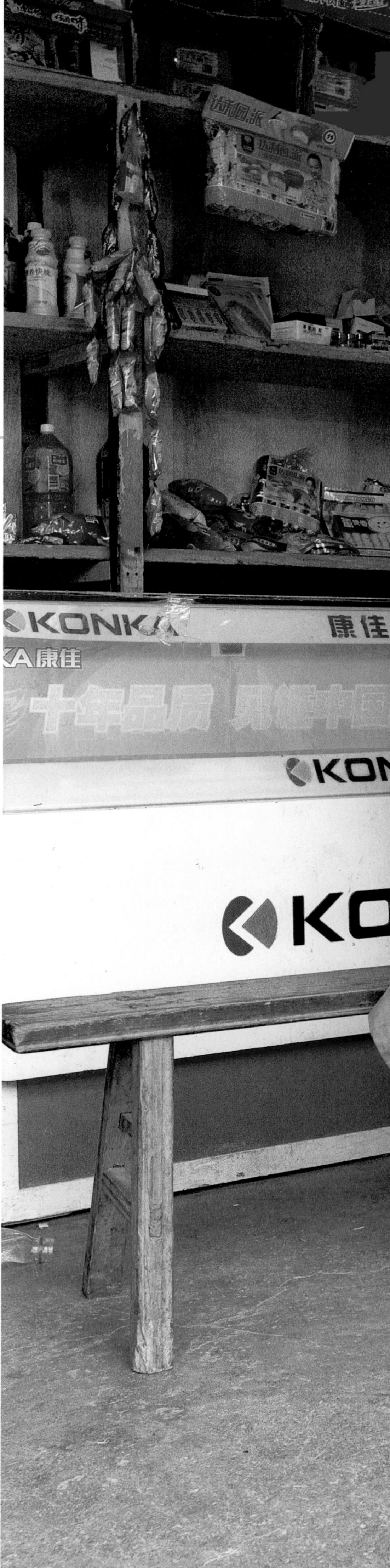

RIGHT Tibetans working at a roadside stall on the highway from Chengdu to Xiaojin in Sichuan province.
RICHARD MCLAREN

18
小角
鶴牌

FOLLOWING PAGES During the Long March, the Red Army stayed in and around the Tibetan village of Zhuokeji, Sichuan province. Mao Zedong, Zhou Enlai, Zhu De and other key Communist leaders spent a week camped out in a palace on their way north to Huining and eventually Yan'an.

RICHARD MCLAREN

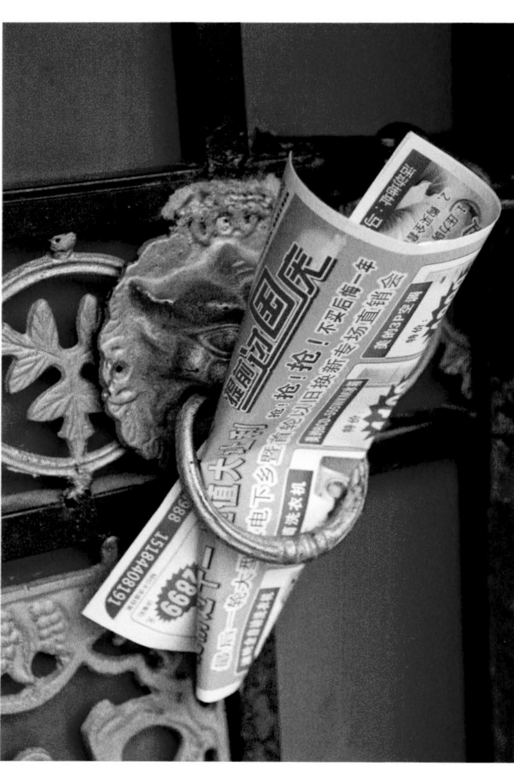

ABOVE A traditional decorative gate latch in the town of Maerkang holds some very modern advertising.

RICHARD MCLAREN

RIGHT A grandmother shares a special moment with her grandson in Baoxing county, Sichuan province.

RICHARD MCLAREN

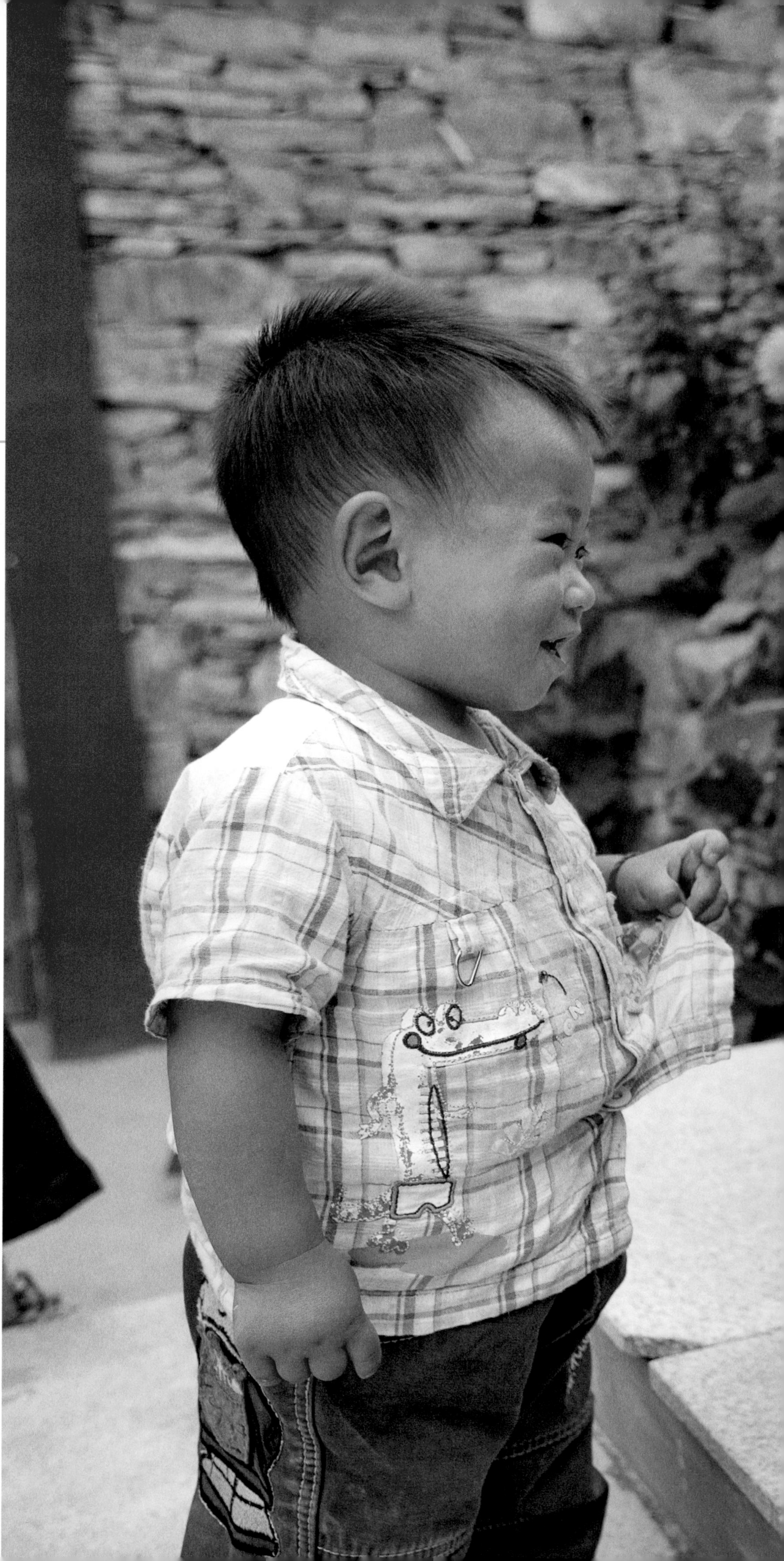

ABOVE A shoe repairman gets to work along the main street of Hongyuan, Sichuan province.
LEO MEIER

LEFT Three chefs take a break outside their restaurant in Maerkang.
RICHARD MCLAREN

FAR LEFT A monk in the town of Xiaojin, Sichuan province, takes time out to play basketball.
RICHARD MCLAREN

ABOVE The groom proposes a toast to guests at a Tibetan wedding celebration in Maerkang.

RICHARD MCLAREN

LEFT A Tibetan villager in the town of Zhuokeji, Sichuan province, prepares fresh peppercorns for drying.

RICHARD MCLAREN

RIGHT A selection of Sichuan herbs and spices for sale in Maerkang.
RICHARD MCLAREN

FOLLOWING PAGES A chef prepares dishes over a wood-burning stove at a small roadside eatery on the highway between Shuajingsi and Maerkang.
RICHARD MCLAREN

ABOVE The Hongyuan–Rou'ergai Grassland was known as the Great Grasslands when the Red Army passed through here in 1935. Covering approximately 11,500 square miles (30,000 square kilometers), it is one of China's three largest wetlands, and home to numerous nomadic Tibetan tribes.
LEO MEIER

RIGHT There's more than just grass in the Hongyuan–Rou'ergai Grassland. It is also home to wildflowers, primitive forests, valley farmlands, lakes, rivers and migrant birds.
LEO MEIER

RIGHT A Tibetan woman in Hongyuan shows off a necklace made from red coral, a traditional trading item among Tibetans.
LEO MEIER

FOLLOWING PAGES A mass of prayer flags has been hung out in Waqie, south of the town of Rou'ergai.
LEO MEIER

ABOVE This row of stationary prayer wheels stands in the village of Dongge, Sichuan province.

LEO MEIER

LEFT A local Tibetan man in the streets of Hongyuan.

LEO MEIER

LEFT Berries known as *sha ji* brighten up a tree in Dongge village. The plant is particularly suited to the dry conditions found in parts of western China, and the berries are used to make fruit drinks and herbal remedies.

LEO MEIER

FOLLOWING PAGES This young man and his family now live in a permanent dwelling close to Hongyuan. However, the former nomads have not lost their love of the Grassland, and every summer from May to August they move into a tent made from woven yak hair about six miles (10 kilometers) out of town to tend to a small herd of yaks.

MICHAEL YOUNG

RIGHT Tibetan farmers come in from the surrounding grasslands to Hongyuan to buy supplies and treats for their children.
LEO MEIER

BELOW A young girl in Hongyuan.
LEO MEIER

LEFT AND BELOW These Tibetan youngsters and their family offer horse rides for tourists in the Hongyuan–Rou'ergai Grassland. In the past a family like this one would have been nomads, but now they live in a permanent dwelling in a settlement near the town of Hongyuan.
MICHAEL YOUNG

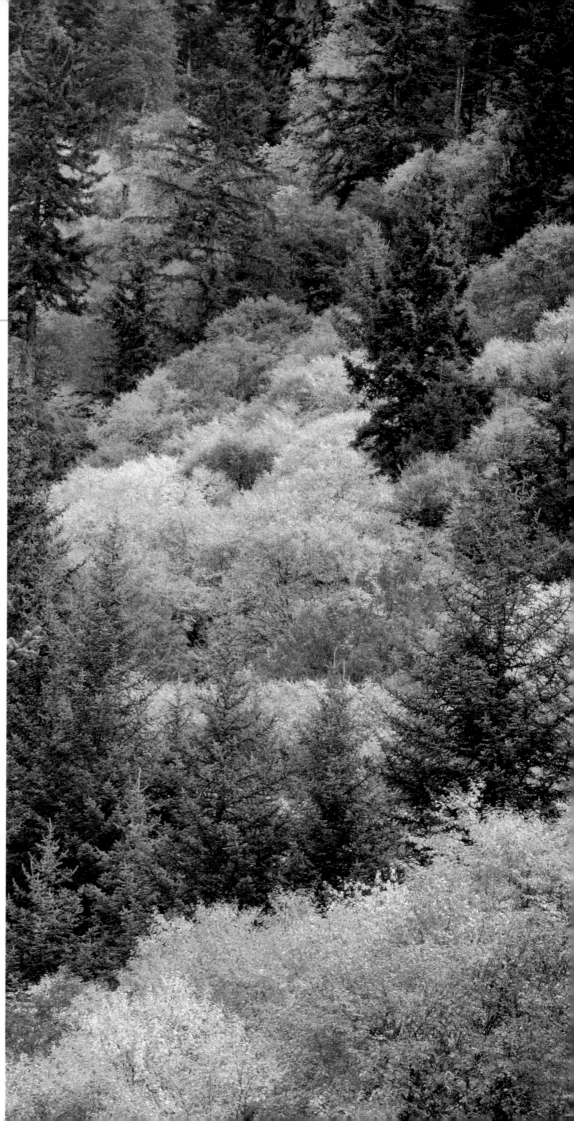

PREVIOUS PAGES Herds tended by nomads graze the grasslands near Rou'ergai. Reaching an altitude of 12,800 feet (3,900 meters), this area is one of the world's largest high-altitude wetlands. It is of global importance for its role in water storage and supply, and for its absorption of carbon dioxide.
LEO MEIER

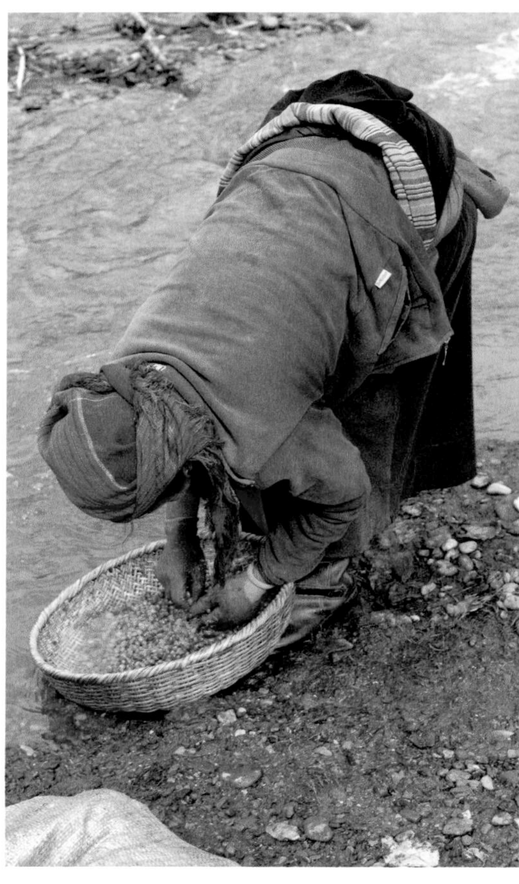

ABOVE A woman washes a basket of *sha ji* on the road between Rou'ergai and Diebu.
LEO MEIER

RIGHT As summer turns to fall and temperatures begin to drop, the forests of Diebu county experience an explosion of colors.
LEO MEIER

PREVIOUS PAGES This Tibetan herdsman has come to Hongyuan for supplies. A growing number of traditionally nomadic people in western China have moved into towns, though many still maintain their herding and grazing practices.
LEO MEIER

BELOW This domesticated yak lives in a stable on the ground floor of a traditional Jiarong Tibetan dwelling near the village of Zhuokeji .
MICHAEL YOUNG

RIGHT A Tibetan herdswoman on the road from Hongyuan to Rou'ergai.

LEO MEIER

LEFT The Hongyuan–Rou'ergai Grassland remains largely unchanged since the time when the Red Army struggled through this area on the Long March.

LEO MEIER

RIGHT This market stall in Hongyuan offers an abundance of fruit and vegetables. One of the great changes of the past 20 years has been the wide variety of fresh produce now available in the Grassland, thanks to growing trade, better roads and higher living standards.
LEO MEIER

ABOVE Children review their lessons outside their school in Hongyuan.
LEO MEIER

RIGHT The handle on a gate in the town of Rou'ergai.
LEO MEIER

RIGHT AND BELOW A Tibetan woman in the Hongyuan–Rou'ergai Grassland spreads out dried yak milk to make cheese. On her waist is a traditional piece of jewelry that doubles as a hook to hold her bucket when she is milking yaks.
LEO MEIER

FOLLOWING PAGES On the northern edge of the Hongyuan–Rou'ergai Grassland, the gently rolling terrain dramatically transforms into a mountain range that marks the border between Sichuan and Gansu provinces.
LEO MEIER

CHAPTER 12

Energy in the Northwest

Struggling out of the mire of the Great Grasslands, the Red Army set out across the bleak landscape of Gansu province. After enduring a year of unimaginable suffering and death, they now faced one more great engagement with the enemy: the battle for Lazikou Pass. Once through the pass, the consolidation of the disparate strands of the Long March could begin.

Although the forbidding landscape of Gansu and the neighboring Ningxia Hui Autonomous Region remains, the economy has come a long way since the days of the Long March. The Hexi Corridor, a string of oases between ridges along the northern edge of the Tibetan Plateau, is known as "the throat of China"—a route that was often taken by invaders from Central Asia.

These days the wind is the most troublesome intrusion. For much of the time it blows steadily, whipping at the earth. A fine, brown dust called loess, the dried remains of Ice Age riverbeds and glacial deposits, assaults the eyes. Packed into topsoil, loess can be highly fertile, but it demands intensive management. Farmers need power to pump water and run agricultural machinery.

LEFT China's ever-expanding road system, including Highway G22 near Huining, Gansu province, has cut travel times dramatically, boosting commerce and giving people the chance to travel to the far corners of the country.

HUI HUAIJIE

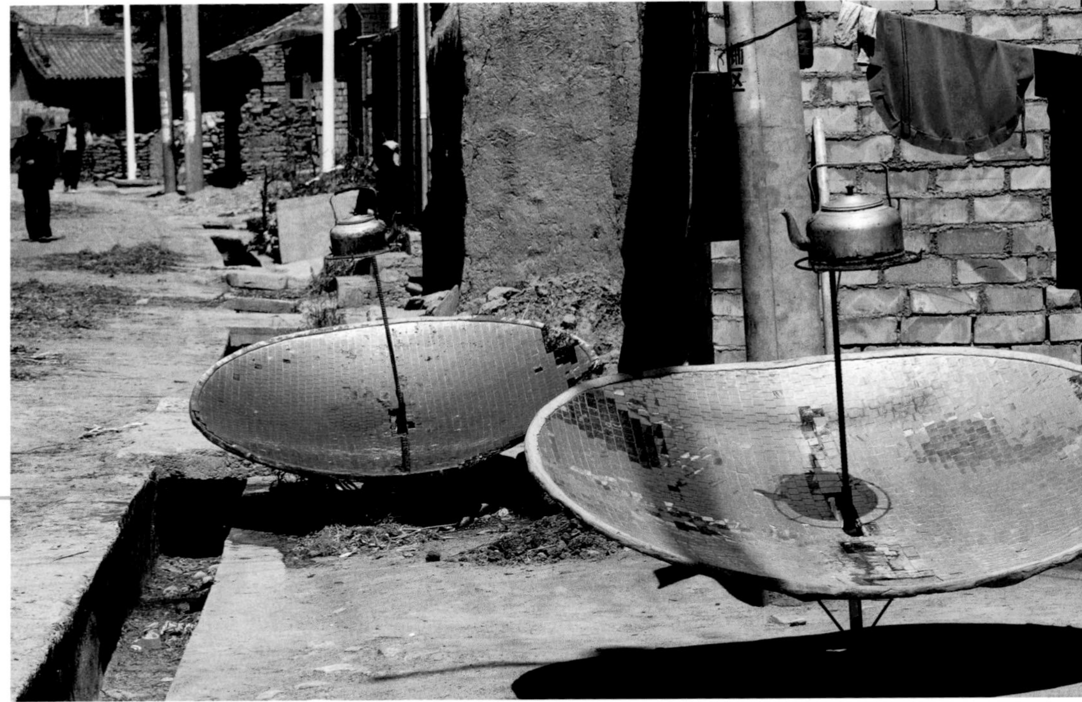

ABOVE The people of Gansu province have found clever ways to capture the sun's energy. These reflective parabolic water boilers in Minxian were supplied by the local government.
MICHAEL YOUNG

RIGHT This striking spire in Huining sits atop a mosque. Huining, where the three main armies of the Long March came together in October 1936, has a small Muslim population. In all, China has an estimated 20 million followers of Islam.
MICHAEL YOUNG

FAR RIGHT A rural teacher in Tian Shui, Gansu province, prepares his lessons for the day.
HUI HUAIJIE

As it turns out, the often-merciless winds are pushing the region into the forefront of alternative energy development. The Gansu Wind Farm is the most striking example. A group of large wind-driven turbines under construction in western Gansu, it is the world's largest wind power project. Its output is expected to reach 20,000 megawatts by 2020, at an estimated cost of RMB 120 billion (US$18.8 billion)

As well, energy will soon be available to Gansu and Ningxia from a huge solar power installation in nearby Qinghai province. A 20-megawatt photovoltaic power plant, by far the largest in the world, is under construction in the

vast desert of the Qaidam Basin. These and other renewable energy projects will go a long way to alleviating concerns about China's heavy reliance on carbon-dioxide-emitting coal-fired power plants.

The population in northwest China is sparse—Gansu has 189 people per square mile (490 per square kilometer). Incomes are still low, though steady progress is being made. Gansu's key industries include petroleum and chemicals, non-ferrous metals mining, heavy machinery manufacturing, electronics and pharmaceuticals. Gansu's per-capita income nearly tripled between 2000 and 2009 to RMB 12,856 (US$2,020). In the same period, Ningxia has increased per-capita income fourfold to RMB 21,475 (US$3,370).

The Ningxia Hui Autonomous Region is home to the Muslim Hui minority, one of 56 ethnic groups officially recognized in China. The Hui are notable for the fact that, although they are related to China's Han majority, their Mandarin includes many Persian and Arabic words.

Formerly part of Gansu province, the autonomous region has the third smallest level of economic output in China. Nevertheless, local authorities remain optimistic, seeing "vast prospects" in energy, agriculture and tourism.

This area shares with Guizhou a powerful ally in Beijing: former Gansu resident Hu Jintao. In 1968, Mao Zedong saw benefits in shipping students of the urban bourgeoisie to the countryside "to learn from the broad masses." Hu, a hydraulic engineering student whose father was persecuted for running a teashop and was thus a member of the suspect petit bourgeois class, volunteered to go to Gansu to work on a hydroelectric power project.

Six years later, Hu, by then a graduate, became the Communist Youth League's

LEFT Today, Hadapu is filled with the spirit of the Long March, with monuments, plaques and a Long March museum, as well as more modern amenities, such as this mobile phone shop.
HUI HUAIJIE

Gansu branch secretary. Tireless travel in his work earned him the nickname in Beijing as "Gansu's walking map." Acclaimed at 40 as the Politburo's youngest member, he became China's President in 2003.

Since then, Hu has been a key supporter of China's onrushing development, especially in the western provinces. Dr. Robert Lawrence Kuhn, a corporate strategist and investment banker who has worked on special projects with China's leadership, quotes an unnamed senior leader who draws an analogy between China's development and constructing roads: "Before Deng Xiaoping, there were no roads; in fact, people didn't think they needed roads. Deng changed people's thinking about roads; he struggled to build some dirt roads.

"Then Jiang Zemin [China's president from 1993 to 2003] converted the dirt roads into paved highways, even though when he began some people still did not believe that roads were the right things to have. Now Hu Jintao is enlarging the highways into expressways and reducing the pollution of the vehicles that travel them."

Dating back more than 2,000 years, the Silk Road passed through Gansu and Ningxia as it linked China with western Asia, the Indian subcontinent and the Mediterranean. Chinese silk was just one of the goods traded along the route—others included glass, precious metals, ceramics, carpets, animals and food.

BELOW Despite dry and harsh conditions, Ningxia Hui Autonomous Region has developed its agricultural sector with the help of extensive irrigation. These farm laborers are hard at work in Xi Ji county.
HUI HUAIJIE

ABOVE These women are selling *huang qi*, a Chinese herbal medicine said to improve digestion, in Dang Chang county, Gansu province.
HUI HUAIJIE

LEFT Muslim students chant scriptures at the Tongxin Grand Mosque in the Ningxia Hui Autonomous Region. The 600-year-old mosque, which was built during the Ming Dynasty, stands as a symbol of China's long history of religious diversity.
HUI HUAIJIE

FOLLOWING PAGES On the road between Hadapu and Minxian, Gansu province, an elderly farmer watches over wheat that has been harvested and laid out on racks for drying.
MICHAEL YOUNG

ABOVE A member of the Hui Muslim minority watches a traditional Peking opera at the Shan Yi Tang Mosque in Xi Ji county, Ningxia Hui Autonomous Region.
HUI HUAIJIE

LEFT A group of retirees join in a game of gateball in Huining.
HUI HUAIJIE

RIGHT A student from Hanwang Central Primary School, Hanwang, Gansu province.
HUI HUAIJIE

FOLLOWING PAGES A shopkeeper in the town of Longxi, Gansu province, offers a selection of cured meats. The sign behind him reads: "The great bearded man and his famous smoked meats." Longxi cured meats are sold as far away as Lanzhou, Xinjiang and Xi'an.
HUI HUAIJIE

大胡子腊肉

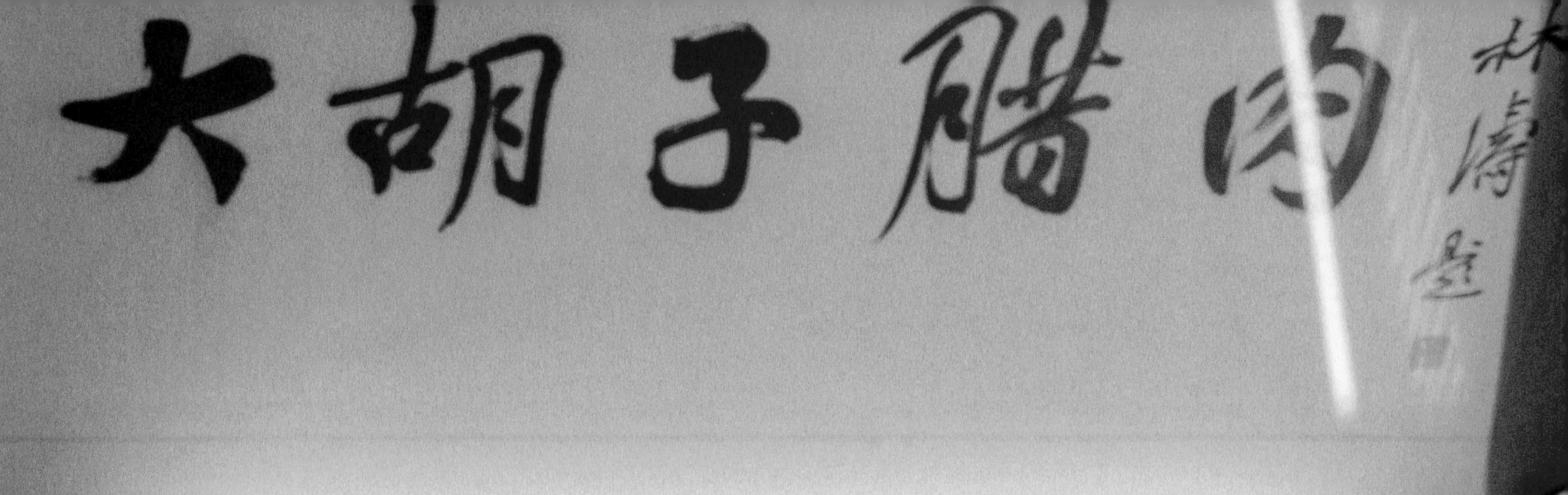
大胡子腊肉

LEFT This Buddhist nun lives in the simple dwelling behind her, near the town of Minxian, Gansu province. The first Buddhist nuns in China were ordained in AD 433.
HAROLD WELDON

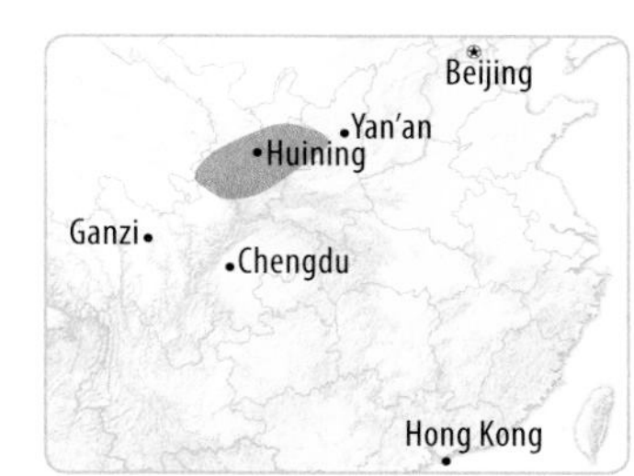

BELOW Goats are herded along the main road of the village of Tong'an, Gansu province.

HUI HUAIJIE

FOLLOWING PAGES The Liupan Mountains extend southward from the Ningxia Hui Autonomous Region, across the eastern edge of Gansu province and into western Shaanxi province.

HUI HUAIJIE

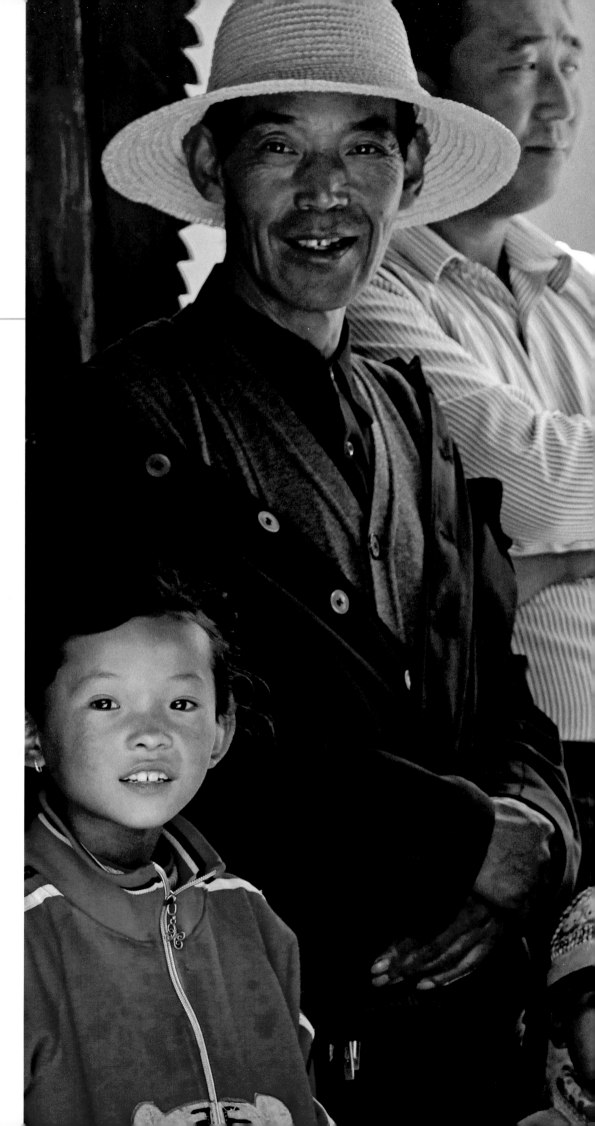

RIGHT Children mix with the older generations in Hadapu, Gansu province. The village played a decisive role in the Long March. The First Front Army stopped here to rest after crossing the Great Grasslands, then decided to push on into northern Shaanxi.

MICHAEL YOUNG

ABOVE This mud brick dwelling in Hadapu was rebuilt in the original style of houses from the time of the Ming Dynasty.

MICHAEL YOUNG

FOLLOWING PAGES Farmers tend to their fields south of the town of Minxian, Gansu province.

MICHAEL YOUNG

CHAPTER 13

The Spirit of Yan'an

The Long March ended in Huining on October 22, 1936, but the fighting didn't. In 1937 Communist and Nationalist forces came together to form the Second United Front to confront the Japanese invader. It was an uneasy alliance, and hostilities between the long-time enemies persisted.

When the Red Army moved its base eastward from Huining to Yan'an, the GMD set up a blockade, cutting supplies. To protect themselves from bombing, first by the Japanese and later by the Nationalists, many revolutionaries lived in rough shelters fashioned from caves dug into the hillsides of Yan'an.

The Communist Party and Red Army high command remained here for ten years, often struggling to keep themselves fed and armed. Muffins made from elm-tree leaves were often substituted for rice. As supplies of arms and ammunition dwindled, the Red Army had to make its own weapons. In Yan'an, grenades were fashioned in backyard potteries.

LEFT With the harvest, autumn is a busy time for farmers, including this woman who is working the fields in the village of Cao Bian near Yan'an, Shaanxi province.
SONG GANGMING

LEFT Two boys hang out at a millstone for grinding grain in Ansai, Shaanxi province. Wheat is the staple of this region, with Shaanxi producing more than 4 million tons a year.
SONG GANGMING

Loess, the dried soil that plagues the north, was one of the Red Army's early problems during this time. Winds blew away the loess, a serious impediment to farming, and dust filled the revolutionaries' cave homes and sometimes made breathing difficult.

A German visitor to the area around 1920 reported dust deposits up to 1,000 feet (300 meters) thick covering 375,000 square miles (970,000 square kilometers). Today, thanks to soil and water conservation and reforestation programs, this vast loess plain has been cut in half, though the struggle continues. A US$525 million program launched in 2000 has cut eroded soil by 60 million tons a year and doubled the area's wheat yield. In the words of a Shaanxi government release, the region has gone "from barren to barn."

Thanks to irrigation and wind barriers, cereals, cotton, tea, tobacco and fruit now grow in abundance. Perhaps Shaanxi's most surprising agricultural product is grape wine. China is the world's seventh largest wine producer and some of the country's finest whites come from Shaanxi.

The province's main resource, however, is coal: Shaanxi is one of the three northwestern Chinese provinces with combined coal reserves of more than 150 billion tons.

Local trade and industry will receive a major boost from the high-speed rail services that will be part of planned rail links to Central and South Asia and Europe. According to Wang Mengshu of the Chinese Academy of Engineering, one of the project's senior consultants, this modern-day Silk Road will deliver passengers and freight on "trains [that] run almost as fast as airplanes."

The Chinese section of one of these networks is expected to run 2,566 miles (4,131 kilometers) through Shanxi, Shaanxi, Gansu, Ningxia, Qinghai and Xinjiang. A second project would carry trains from China through Russia and into Europe's railway system via Germany. A third line would extend south to connect China with Vietnam, Burma, Thailand and Malaysia. Eventually, says Wang, passengers would be able to travel from London to Beijing in two days and then on to Singapore in another day.

Founded as a frontier post during the Sui dynasty (581–618), Yan'an was given its current name in 1369. The first part of the name comes from the Yan River on which it lies. "Yan" translates as "extend" or "prolong," and "an" as "peace," so Yan'an could be said to mean "Eternal Peace."

BELOW Schoolchildren in Ansai join in the traditional Ansai waist drum dance. Marked by vigorous drumming, singing, flag-waving and even gymnastics, this lively dance dates back more than two thousand years. It is believed to have started as a military warning system, but later evolved into a folk dance in which people asked the gods for blessings and good harvests.
SONG GANGMING

The Western Development Strategy has had a dramatic impact on Shaanxi's highway system, which has grown more than ten-fold from less than 125 miles (200 kilometers) in 1999 to more than 1,500 miles (2,500 kilometers) today. The automotive industry has grown hand in hand with the expanding road network. The Shaanxi Automobile Group based in Xi'an City manufactures trucks, buses and minivans that are sold across China and in more than 30 other countries.

Yan'an and Xi'an have both benefited from the rise of China's new middle class. Shaanxi abounds in history—most notably, more than 100 sites in Yan'an associated with the Red Army's early years and the 8,000-man terracotta army at the tomb of China's first emperor, Qin Shi Huangdi, east of Xi'an. They attract affluent tourists in increasing numbers, from across China and overseas.

The Yan'an Revolutionary Museum, which offers displays on the last stages of the Long March, and the area's cave houses draw more than four million visitors a year. Exhibits include a four-cave complex where Mao lived and worked. Mao's canopy bed is littered with cigarette butts, illustrating the long hours he spent planning the ongoing struggles against the Japanese and the Guomindang.

To accommodate the growing number of tourists, hotels sprout almost monthly. Xi'an alone has more than

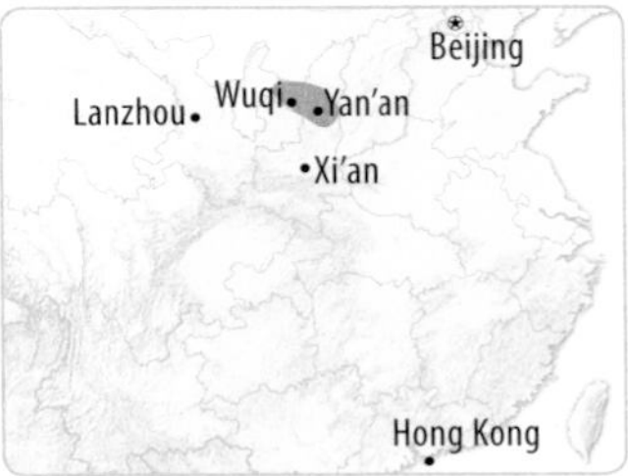

LEFT Members of a Yan'an street theater troupe gather to perform a northern Shaanxi folk dance called *shaan bei yangko.*
SONG GANGMING

RIGHT The Yan'an Red Army base historical site has become a popular stop on "Red Tour" trips along the route of the Long March. Items for sale at the base include satchel bags featuring images of Mao Zedong and the slogan "Serve the People."
SONG GANGMING

LEFT Two young boys at home in Ansai.
SONG GANGMING

100 hotels. One of the most recent is a Westin Hotel that includes a museum displaying "the world's only suit of armor crafted entirely from gold."

The region's exalted role in China's history seems to enliven local spirits. On a visit to Yan'an not long after the Long Marchers had arrived, American author and journalist Theodore White wrote about the town's "bustle and excitement, pitched to the sound of shrill bugles echoing and rebounding from the hills."

Today the Long Marchers' vitality lives on. Says Professor Liu Shuangping of Ningxia University's Economic Institute: "West China is like the sun between 8:00 and 9:00 a.m.—full of youthful spirit and promise."

PREVIOUS PAGES China's older generation has witnessed astonishing changes in the span of a single lifetime—civil war, hardship, upheaval and finally ever-increasing prosperity. This Ansai family relaxes over a game of *wu zi qi*, also known as gobang, in which players try to lay down black and white pieces in a set order.

SONG GANGMING

RIGHT Yan'an has grown into a vibrant city, with the petroleum, coal, energy and chemical sectors forming the cornerstone of the local economy. This street cleaner works for the local government in Yan'an.

SONG GANGMING

安环卫

LEFT This Long March monument in Wuqi, Shaanxi province, presents a striking silhouette with the sun behind it.
SONG GANGMING

FOLLOWING PAGES Once an isolated rural center, Yan'an has become a bustling city where the older generations of farmers and a growing middle class live side by side. This elderly resident is passing an outdoor fashion show that is promoting the opening of a new shopping center.

SONG GANGMING

BELOW This market selling boxes of snacks and biscuits provides a colorful sight along a suburban street in Yan'an.

SONG GANGMING

亲，时尚之城即将绽放 Hold住
专线：25

ABOVE Even the latest fashions in eyewear are available in Yan'an these days.
SONG GANGMING

LEFT At this country fair in Zhidan county, Shaanxi province, tourists can have their photo taken with two of Asia's best known—and most endangered—species, the giant panda and Bengal tiger.
SONG GANGMING

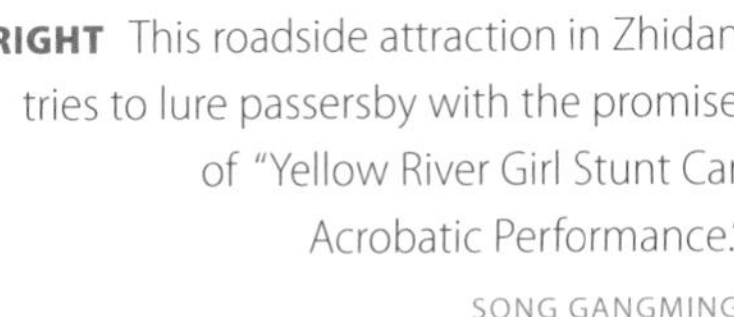

RIGHT This roadside attraction in Zhidan tries to lure passersby with the promise of "Yellow River Girl Stunt Car Acrobatic Performance."
SONG GANGMING

FOLLOWING PAGES Women gather in Long March Plaza in Wuqi to perform a fan dance as part of their morning exercises.
SONG GANGMING

杂技表演
飞车专用
飞车女郎：佳佳丽 邓婷梦
山西黄河女子 汽车飞车 特技表演团
售票处
成人10元
儿童5元
世界绝技 惊险刺激 值得一看 一定要看
黄河女子 汽车
全场表演绝对比世界
惊险、更刺激、更具有观
罕见的节目。

PREVIOUS PAGES The leaders of the Long March continue to watch over Yan'an. Following in the spirit of the Long March, China's next generation can look forward to a bright future.
SONG GANGMING

RIGHT Cave dwellings remain a source of housing in Ansai, north of Yan'an, just as they were when the Red Army arrived in the area more than seven decades ago. Dug into hillsides of tightly packed loess soil, the houses are easy and cheap to construct, and the natural insulation of the earth makes them warm in winter and cool in summer.
MICHAEL YOUNG

ABOVE The Victory monument in Wuqi celebrates the end of the Long March. This boy is standing at the top of a timeline of the major events during the Long March, starting with the red star at the far end. With more than 350 sites related to the Long March and the Chinese revolution, Yan'an and Wuqi have become major tourist attractions.
SONG GANGMING

LEFT Wang Zewei is well known in the Ansai area for singing the folk songs of Shaanxi province.

MICHAEL YOUNG

ABOVE Paper cutouts are an important part of Shaanxi's cultural heritage. Using only a pair of scissors and a piece of paper, artisans create stunning geometric patterns that often tell significant folk stories. This cutout, created in Ansai, celebrates the Year of the Rabbit.

MICHAEL YOUNG

拍云崖暖，大渡桥横铁索寒。
更喜岷山千里雪，三军过后尽开颜。

毛泽东

一九六二年四月六日

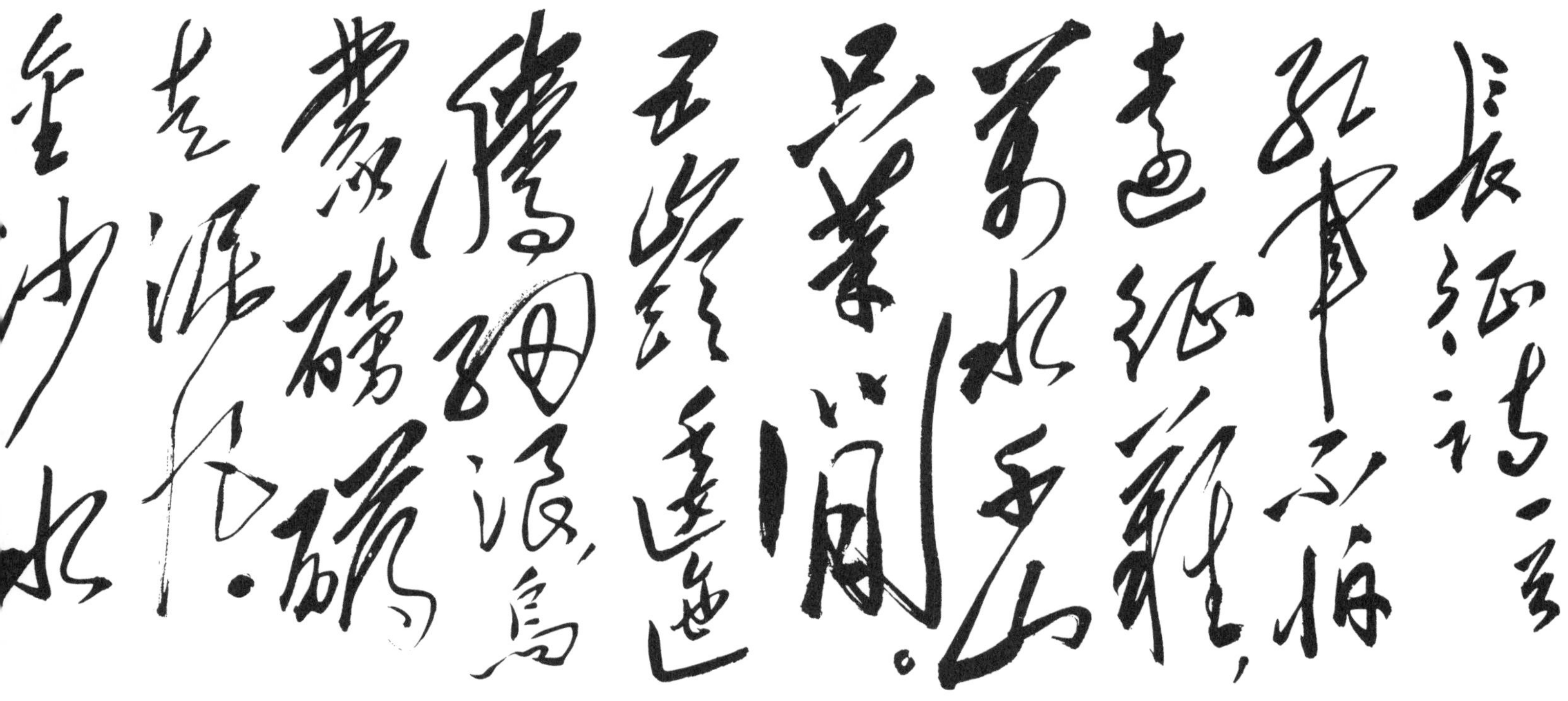

The Red Army fears not the trials of the March,

Holding light ten thousand crags and torrents.

The Five Ridges wind like gentle ripples

And the majestic Wumeng roll by, globules of clay.

Warm the steep cliffs lapped by the waters of Golden Sand,

Cold the iron chains spanning the Dadu River.

Minshan's thousand li of snow joyously crossed,

The three Armies march on, each face glowing.

The Long March by Mao Zedong
Mao's original calligraphy for The Long March is shown above

Nikon

BEHIND THE SCENES

The History of the Project

This book has its origins in another volume published by Weldon International more than 25 years ago. *China: The Long March* commemorated the 50th anniversary of the Long March by sending some of the world's greatest photographers to retrace the route.

At the time, Harold Weldon, a 19-year-old assistant to photographer Leo Meier, and Li Dong, an interpreter and liaison representative for the Chinese members of the project, were part of the survey team that traveled the entire route, gathering logistical information and researching locations for the final shoot.

A New Era, a New Book

In late 2010 the Ministry responsible for publishing in China, the General Administration of Press and Publications, gave their support to a new book that would celebrate the people and places along the Long March route today. Once again world-class photographers would be enlisted—ten chosen by the Chinese Photographers' Association and four foreign photographers.

In April 2011 Qingdao Publishing Group signed a co-publishing agreement with the Australian publisher, Weldon International. The project was officially launched in the city of Qingdao at a ceremony hosted by Mr. Meng Mingfei, Chairman of Qingdao Publishing Group, and Mr. Gao Jimin, Deputy Editor-in-Chief of Qingdao Publishing Group. Guests included officials from the General Administration of Press and Publications and the Qingdao City Government; Mr. Li Qun, Party Secretary of the Qingdao City Government; former Australian Prime Minister the Hon. R. J. Hawke; Dr. Geoff Raby, Australian Ambassador to China at the time; and Weldon International Chairman Kevin Weldon.

In mid-2011 Harold Weldon and Li Dong set out with a new

LEFT Harold Weldon was surrounded by locals when the 1985 survey team visited the town of Minxian, Gansu province. "We journeyed through many regions that had rarely if ever been visited by Westerners," Harold recalls. "In all these regions we were constantly struck by the spirit of the local people—wherever we went the strength, beauty and courage of the Chinese people shone through."

LEO MEIER

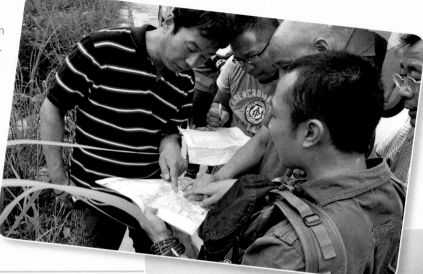

RIGHT Stopping near the Dadu River, Sichuan province, Team Leader Li Dong goes over the route ahead with the survey team. During the survey trip this region was inundated with torrential rainfall, causing dangerous landslides and rockfalls.
MICHAEL YOUNG

survey team retracing the full route of the Long March in preparation for the final shoot. The team encountered landslides, extreme temperatures and high altitudes on a demanding 6,000-mile (10,000-kilometer) journey through eight provinces in 35 days.

RIGHT Harold and his nephew Michael Young look over the Dadu River near the town of Shimian, Sichuan province. The journey had special significance because Michael was 19, the same age that Harold had been on the 1985 survey trip.
REN JIE

The Photoshoot

On September 16, 2011, the photographers gathered for their briefing in Beijing, and left soon after for their individual journeys along sections of the Long March route. They visited places of rugged beauty, diverse history and culture, and immense natural resources. The photographers recorded that some areas had changed little since the Red Army passed through over 75 years ago, while others had undergone dramatic development.

It was not always easy going—two photographers were delayed by landslides caused by record rainfall and two others were involved in car accidents, though fortunately no one was injured.

In all, the team took more than 20,000 photographs, representing an amazing portrait of the people, the towns and cities, and the landscapes they visited.

At the end of the seven-day shoot, all the photographs were transferred onto hard drives at the Weldon office in Beijing and transported to the photoediting team in Australia.

With this book, we hope to convey the spirit of the Chinese people who continue to drive the Long March forward, and to recognize the achievements of those men and women who undertook the original Long March so many years ago.

RIGHT After completing the Long March journey 26 years ago, Li Dong, the youngest Chinese member of the survey team, was honored to meet Madame Kang Keqing, the widow of Long March commander General Zhu De. When Mme. Kang Keqing asked Li Dong for his impressions and thoughts after completing the Long March, he quickly replied: "Those heroes who were part of the original Long March are entitled to do whatever they want in life. They endured and survived so much hardship that it gave them the skills to overcome obstacles and achieve their goals for the rest of their lives."
MICHAEL YOUNG

LEFT AND ABOVE The 2011 survey team gathers at a momument marking the end of the Long March in Wuqi, Shaanxi province. In 1985 Harold had given a speech at the same place to a crowd of curious locals who had never seen a Westerner, or heard one talk.

MICHAEL YOUNG (LEFT), LEO MEIER (ABOVE)

RIGHT One memorable moment on the 2011 survey trip happened when the team visited the site of the first river crossing of the Long March in Yudu county, Jiangxi province. When a group of 20 Red Army choir singers, who were grandchildren of Long March veterans, saw the replica Red Army caps being worn by members of the team, they broke into a chorus of Long March songs.

XIAO ZHONG REN

LEFT The survey team visited numerous schools along the way. At this a middle school in the town of Zunyi, Michael is surrounded by a mob of children excited by the intriguing visitors.

HAROLD WELDON

LEFT AND BELOW In the remote town of Hongyuan, in the Hongyuan–Rou'ergai Grassland in northern Sichuan province, the team tracked down a yak herdsman they had met in 1985. Twenty-six years ago the herdsman led a nomadic life in the grasslands. Today he lives in a permanent home in Hongyuan and keeps a small herd of yaks.

REN JIE (LEFT), MICHAEL YOUNG (BELOW)

ABOVE AND LEFT Harold and Li Dong show the herdsman and his family the daily logbook Harold kept during the 1985 survey trip, which included a photograph of Harold and the herdsman.

REN JIE

RIGHT Harold and Li Dong shake hands at the highest point of the Jiajin pass—an altitude of over 13,500 feet (4,100 meters). The Red Army passed this point during their arduous crossing of the Great Snow Mountains in 1935.

MICHAEL YOUNG

LEFT In 1985 when the survey team visited Hongyuan, they were greeted by excited schoolchildren who had never seen a foreigner. "They followed us everywhere," Harold recalls. "All that day I had three children hanging off each of my arms!" During the 2011 trip to the region, Li Dong tracked down six of the original children. "An unforgettable moment for me was when I walked into the town of Hongyuan," Harold says of his meeting with them. "I was met by a group of men and women, bright faces, smiling, laughing and running toward me. It was great to see them now in their late 30s with families and successful careers of their own."

MICHAEL YOUNG

ABOVE The calligraphy shown on the back cover says "The New Long March" and is an example of floor calligraphy, which is known as Di Shu in China. Floor calligraphy is a new way of practicing calligraphy where the characters are painted on the ground with water using a brush pen made of sponge. This method is environmentally friendly and more convenient, and has encouraged more people to learn calligraphy. The best way to practice this method is to stand up on your toes with your feet shoulder-width apart and keep your legs and waist straight but if you do this for long, you'll need to stretch your elbows and breath deeply to relax.

HOU XILI

ABOVE During the 2011 survey trip the team attracted extensive coverage from Chinese television, radio, newspapers and websites. Here Li Dong discovers a local paper in Zunyi with a feature story on the project.

MICHAEL YOUNG

LEFT Shen Yao, Head of the Design Department of Qingdao Publishing House, paints some calligraphy tests for the book at the production office in Sydney.

HAROLD WELDON

THE PHOTOGRAPHERS

Catherine Croll

COUNTRY Australia
ASSIGNMENT Zunyi–Maotai–Chishui, Guizhou province

Based in Newcastle, Australia, Croll began her career as a music photographer, traveling across Australia, the United States, England and Europe. After working as a lecturer in photography and painting, she embarked on two long tours of China, documenting the country's traditional cultural heritage. Some of that work appeared in her book *China—A Portrait*. Since 2008 she has worked on cultural exchange programs between China and Australia, overseeing exhibitions in both countries.

"While we were documenting the New Long March I often felt as though we were visiting villages that had remained largely the same as when the Red Army passed through 75 years ago," Croll recalls. "The cobbled streets of Tucheng old town and the Ming dynasty village of Bing'an were particularly interesting. Here the local people were friendly, welcoming and inquisitive as foreign visitors are rare. Each day as I looked out over the tranquil farming villages I found it hard to reconcile them with the fierce battles and the thousands of young men and women who had died while crossing this land."

Feng Jianguo

COUNTRY China
ASSIGNMENT Dayong, Hunan province; Tongren–Guiyang, Guizhou province

Feng Jianguo studied photography in Japan, and got his Master of Fine Arts in 1998. Now a professor of photography at the Beijing Film Academy, he specializes in large format black-and-white photographs in the style of Ansel Adams. He has made numerous trips to western China, including Ningxia, Xinjiang, Xizang and Sichuan provinces, photographing both the people and natural environment of the region.

Feng says his assignment gave him a strong sense of the Long March. "Though history does not repeat itself, it indeed leaves footprints on today's life. Walking through the Long March passage again, I experienced the crossover of time and space, many amazing things and many emotional moments. I heartily wish people living along the path may inherit wonderful traditions, live a happy life and march toward a bright future."

Hei Ming

COUNTRY China
ASSIGNMENT Anshun–Liupanshui, Guizhou province; Qujing, Yunnan province

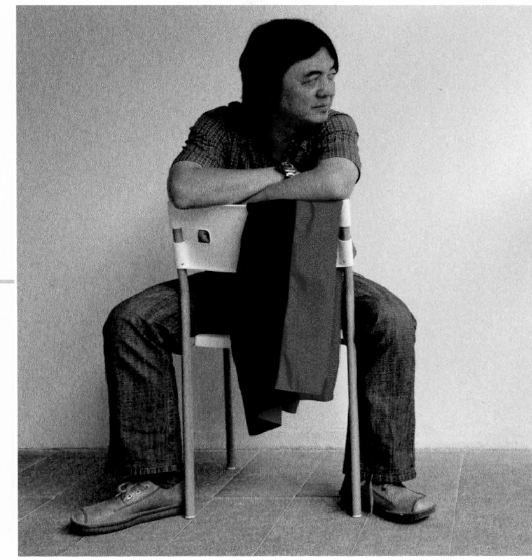

Formerly the director of the photography department of *China Youth*, Hei continues to take photographs for the magazine. He has won numerous photographic and art awards, and his work has been featured in exhibitions in China, the United States, the United Kingdom and France. Hei's photographic books include *Passing the Young Age*, *Walk into the Peking University* and *The Legend of Tibet*.

"The new Long March showed me new images," Hei declares. "Thanks to everyone caught in my camera during the trip!"

LEFT The photographic team at the Temple of Heaven, Beijing, before heading off on their assignments (from left to right): Hui Huaijie, Wang Wenlan, Feng Jianguo, Liu Yingyi, Hei Ming, Shi Yongting, Richard Mclaren, Catherine Croll, Beijing Co-ordinator Laxmi Weldon, Liang Daming, Leo Meier, Liu Shaoning, Song Gangming, Li Fan, Field Interpreter Dong Kai and Project Director Li Dong. Not present: Sebastien Micke.

LEO MEIER

Hui Huaijie

COUNTRY China
ASSIGNMENT Lazikou–Minxian–Huining, Gansu province

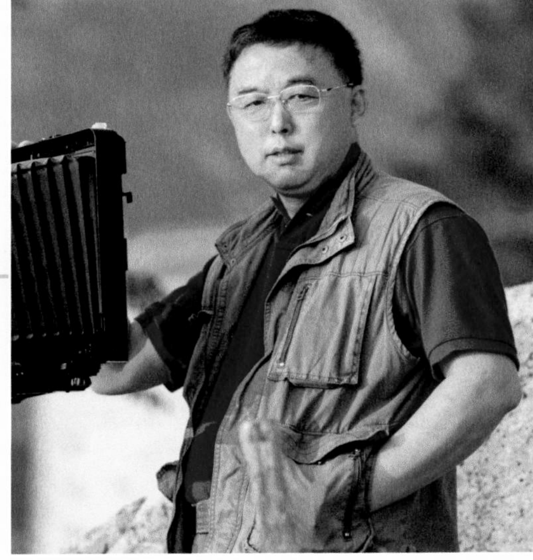

Hui was born in Shaanxi province and has spent more than 20 years photographing the stark land and rugged people of the loess plateau in northwestern China. Many of his photographs have received awards at the National Photographic Exhibition and the China International Photographic Art Exhibition. Hui, who is a member of China Photographers' Association and the China Art Photography Association, was named "Outstanding Earthquake Relief Photographer" in 2008.

"When I traveled along the route of the Long March," he says, "I clicked the shutter time and again, so I could tell people all over the world what had happened there."

Li Fan

COUNTRY China
ASSIGNMENT Danba, Sichuan province

Associate Professor at the Press and Communication College of Shaanxi Normal University, Li is best known as a photographer of the human form. In recent years, he has visited the Liangshan Yi Autonomous Prefecture in Sichuan province 17 times, photographing members of the Yi nationality. His goal is to create a visual memory for the Yi, whose history dates back a thousand years. Li has won numerous awards, including a gold medal at the 20th National Photographic Art Exhibition and silver at the 17th China Press Photography "Golden Camera" Awards.

Li says he has visited Danba before, but the assignment for this book gave him a new perspective on the area. "As the topic is about the Long March, I felt a kind of responsibility and pressure: the responsibility to use my camera to record the changes of the areas since the Red Army left their footprints, and the pressure to produce good photographs in such a tight schedule."

Liang Daming

COUNTRY China
ASSIGNMENT Shimian–Luding, Sichuan province

A teacher at the Beijing Photography Correspondence School and a freelance photographer, Liang is a longstanding director of the China Photography Copyright Association and the China Portrait Photography Society, and a member of the China Photographers' Association and the Professional Photographers of America. He has won numerous awards and had thousands of photographs published, along with the book *Selection of Works of Liang Daming*.

"As I traveled along on the passage of the Long March, the footprint of the history was reflected in my mind through the lens," Liang says. "As I clicked the shutter, all kinds of life was recorded in my heart."

Liu Shaoning

COUNTRY China
ASSIGNMENT Changting, Fujian province; Ruijin–Jinggangshan, Jiangxi province

Lui is party secretary and president of the Anhui branch of China Mobile Communications Group Design Institute, a member of China Photographers' Association, director of the photography branch of the China Communication Association and Vice Chairman of the Anhui Photographers' Association. His recent work, *The Tea House Anecdotes*, received a silver prize at the 5th Imaging China national photography competition and *The New Generation of The Tea House* received a bronze medal at the 23rd National Photographic Art Exhibition.

"I was in charge of shooting the starting point of the Long March—Ruijin, Jiangxi," Liu recalls. "It gave me an opportunity to have a closer look at the history of the Long March, and put great responsibility on my shoulders. Following the footprints of the Red Army, the stories that happened during the Long March kept emerging in my mind. I was stunned to see the great changes that have happened in the area over the years."

Liu Yingyi

COUNTRY China
ASSIGNMENT Guilin, Guangxi Autonomous Region; Liping, Guizhou province

Liu works as a photographer in the News Centre of the Beijing Public Security Bureau's Traffic Administration, and is a member of China Photographers' Association, Vice President of the Beijing Photographers' Association and director of Photographic Committee of the National Public Security and Art Federation. He has won more than 100 awards, most notably the China Photographic Gold Medal, China's highest photographic award. Liu's books include *Celebrities and Their Cars* and *My Hutong Life*.

"One of the stops on my trip was Longsheng county, Guangxi province," Liu says. "There I visited not only the famous Dragon's Backbone Rice Terraces, but also Huangluo, a Yao ethnic village known as 'Number One Long Hair Village.' I will never forget the wonderful natural scenery and the sincere people."

Richard Mclaren

COUNTRY United Kingdom/United States
ASSIGNMENT Xiaojin–Lianghekou–Maerkang, Sichuan province

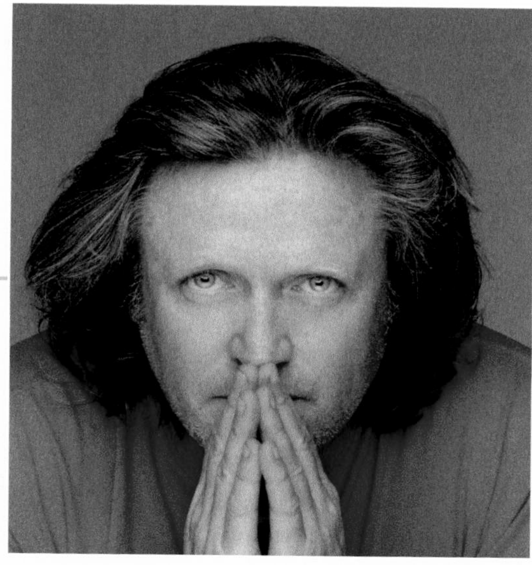

Although British-born Mclaren is based in Los Angeles, his work for magazines, advertisers and other clients has taken him around the world. The long list of countries stamped on his passport includes Brazil, South Africa, Thailand, Australia, Dubai, Bangladesh, Iceland and now, of course, China. His subjects have included Nelson Mandela, Jennifer Lopez, Orlando Bloom and Gwyneth Paltrow, and his work has appeared in such magazines as *GQ, Vogue, Elle, Marie Claire, Esquire, Rolling Stone, Harpers Bazaar* and *Vanity Fair*.

"The most amazing thing I've done in photography so far was shooting Nelson Mandela in the Presidential Palace in South Africa," Mclaren states. "China was the second best thing I've done in my career. It was a photographer's dream. Wherever you pointed the camera, there was an amazing picture to be taken. It was an incredible experience, one I will talk about for the rest of my life."

Leo Meier

COUNTRY Switzerland/Australia
ASSIGNMENT Hongyuan–Rou'ergai, Sichuan province; Diebu, Gansu province

Meier, recognized as one of Australia's leading photographers, has photographed over 20 books, many requiring epic journeys into some of the world's most remote regions. He has also contributed to 29 international books and numerous high-profile magazines, and led a film crew through China for a TV documentary and book about the Red Army under Mao Zedong. Over the years Meier has designed and built a large array of unique and specialized equipment to deal with the special challenges of macro, panorama and stereo photography.

Meier particularly remembers photographing a young woman as she was milking cows in the grasslands of Sichuan province, crouched in mud, alone, far from other people and habitation, doing her daily arduous chores in bitter cold and isolation. "To my astonishment, I could hear the young woman gently sing a beautifully soft and happy song underneath her veil. Despite what in my world would be grounds for discontent, she appeared at peace with herself and the world around her. When I returned home I would show my peers pictures of the remote and exotic places I had visited. But what picture could ever hope to encapsulate and communicate such a precious and humbling experience?"

Sebastien Micke

COUNTRY France/United States
ASSIGNMENT Kunming–Lijiang–Shangri La, Yunnan province

Born in Sète, France, in 1977, Micke took up photography at the age of sixteen. He became a staff photographer for *Paris Match* in 1999, and now works for the magazine out of Los Angeles. Micke's subjects have included President Barack Obama, Mariah Carey and George Clooney, and his work has also been published in *Vanity Fair Italia*, *Vogue Brasil*, *Elle Français*, *Cosmopolitan* and *GQ*.

Micke says he was astounded by the beauty of Yunnan and the simple lives of its people, who remain close to nature. "My fondest memory of this trip was walking in the ancient village of Shangri La. The buildings and temples were relics that transported me to times past. I was no longer in 2011. In this magical place, I was able to have a blessing from a monk in one of the temples. This intimate ceremony will always be one of my greatest spiritual experiences."

Shi Yongting

COUNTRY China
ASSIGNMENT Luding–Xiaojin–Dawei, Sichuan province

Born in Changchun city, Shi developed an interest in photography when he was in middle school. He has spent much of his life photographing China's natural scenery, particularly the ice and snow of Changbai Mountain and the Songhua River in northeastern China. A member of the Chinese Photographers' Association, Shi was named one of China's Top Ten Landscape Photographers in 2001 and has won awards at the 15th and 20th National Photographic Art Exhibitions.

"I will always remember shooting the Tibetan people in the Du Qiao region," he says. "They have their own culture and religion, and it seems that they lead a life based on the laws of nature. They are so truthful and friendly to each other, just like a family. There is no influence from modern high-tech world—I think that must be what we would call heaven."

Song Gangming

COUNTRY China
ASSIGNMENT Yan'an–Wuqi–Ansai, Shaanxi province

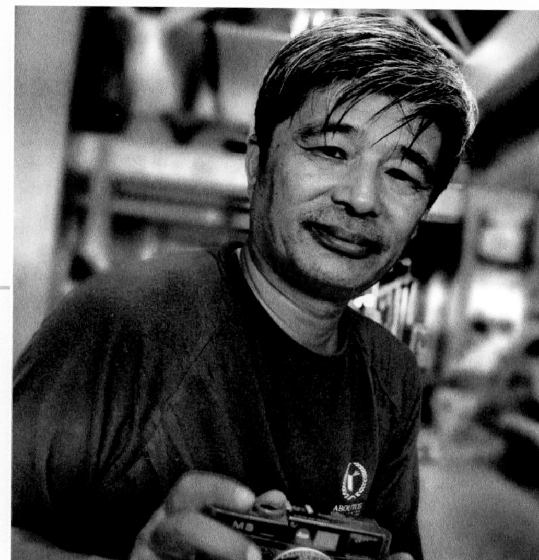

A Visiting Professor of Photography at Wuhan University, Song is Vice President of the Hubei Photographers' Association. He also contributes to *Photography World* and *Hong Kong Pictorial* and is the inventor of a U-type image sensor for digital cameras. Song has won numerous awards, including a Gold Medal at the China Photography Awards.

Song says he approached his assignment with a renewed sense of reverence for the Long March. "I learned about the Long March when I was a child, but to be honest, I had no admiration coming from the bottom of my heart. After getting older and experiencing the ups and downs of life, I developed a deep respect for the Long March. They had accomplished this incredible journey. Pursuing their dreams made them saints. The Long March not only belongs to China, but also to the world."

Wang Wenlan

COUNTRY China
ASSIGNMENT Xichang–Liangshan Mountain, Sichuan province

Wang began his photographic career in the People's Liberation Army in 1974, working for the PLA news report. Over the years he has covered numerous major events, including the Tang Shan earthquake and the 2008 Olympics. Today he is a senior reporter and director of the Photography Department of the *China Daily* and serves as Vice President of the China Photographers' Association. Wang is a consultant to a number of art magazines including *Chinese Photographer* and *Philharmonic*, and teaches courses in news photography at Beijing University, Xinhua News Agency, *People's Daily* and other academic and news institutions. He also contributed to *China: The Long March* 25 years ago.

"The Long March is a great epic," Wang says. "The spirit of it will live on for generations."

THE AUTHORS

Anthony Paul

Anthony Paul has worked as an editor, foreign correspondent and author in the Asia-Pacific region for more than 40 years. As editor-at-large for numerous magazines, including *Fortune, Reader's Digest, Asiaweek* and *Asia Inc.*, he has covered wars in Indochina, Afghanistan and Iraq and written extensively about China's economic rise. A longtime member of London's International Institute for Strategic Studies and honorary life member of the Hong Kong, Tokyo and Bangkok foreign correspondents' clubs, he currently divides his time between Brisbane and Hong Kong, writes a world-affairs column for *The Straits Times*, Singapore, and lectures on Asia-Pacific affairs.

Brodie Paul

Mandarin-speaking Brodie Paul has spent most of his life in Asia, growing up in Hong Kong, studying at Fudan University in Shanghai, and teaching English in Taipei and Dalian, China. He later lived and worked in Shanghai for 10 years, first as Dun & Bradstreet's business development manager, then as a partner in Compradores.com, an online import-export company. Now raising a family in Australia, he works as a trade and investment specialist with the Queensland Government.

RIGHT This soldier, who appears in a painting of the Red Army marching through the Loushan Pass in January 1935 after defeating Nationalist forces, wears his Red Army cap with pride and unbroken determination.
CHINA NATIONAL MUSEUM

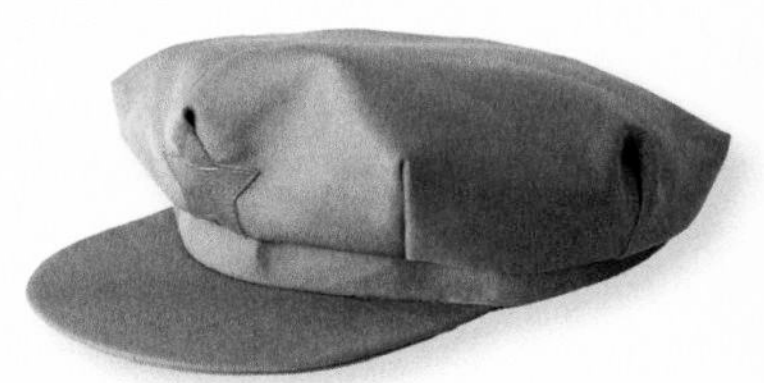

THE RED ARMY CAP

By Wang Teh-ching

From *Stories of the Long March*

The distinctive pale blue, eight-pointed Red Army cap has come to symbolize the spirit and courage of the soldiers of the Long March. Today, replica Red Army caps and uniforms are popular among tourists who wear them on "Red Tours" as they retrace the Long March route. This story shows the significance of the cap to a young Red Army soldier who fought during the Sino-Japanese War of 1937–45.

At the end of October, we were nearing Weitsun, the principal point of supply of the Japanese in attacking Hsinkou and other districts. One pitch-black night we were groping our way into the village along a small lane at the south entrance. It was my first engagement with the enemy and I felt very tense, not knowing how I ought to act. Squad leader Hu Tung-sheng told me to follow him closely. He was a veteran fighter who had taken part in the Long March and everybody trusted him.

"Rat-tat-tat!" an enemy machine gun at the crossroad opened up; bullets whizzed past me. By the flash we could see a corner formed by the wall in front of us. Instead of sheltering himself in this safe nook, the squad leader shoved me in it, pressing himself tight against the outer wall alongside me. The enemy machine gun snapped at us with greater fury, nipping the padding of our sleeves.

Hu kept shooting at the enemy to make them use up more bullets. As day dawned the enemy machine gun became silent. Suddenly Hu turned toward me and said, "Little Wang, make ready to charge!"

Without waiting for my reply he jumped out and dashed forward. I followed him.

As we approached the enemy machine gun, I thought I heard him shout "Off with it!" followed immediately by two deafening shots. In a twinkling, amid the pall of smoke, we were at the enemy. Grappling with one of them, Hu grabbed hold of the machine gun and with a mighty jerk pulled it over. Then he administered a ferocious kick or two at the fellow, who gave a pained squeal and dropped back motionless.

At this instant, there was firing from the left and the squad leader fell, still clutching the machine gun. Horror-stricken, I hurried to lift him and support him against my body, not knowing what to do. (By now, all our troops had entered the village.)

After a while, he raised his head slightly and said, "Little Wang, don't be afraid ..."

A faint smile flickered over his face. With his last ounce of strength he fished out an old worn cap and placed it in my hand. He tried to say something but could not summon up the strength to speak. But I understood what he would have said had he been able.

Squad leader Hu Tung-sheng had been in the habit of telling us the story of his cap. He was a newly enlisted fighter of 16 during the Long March, with a peasant towel tied around his head. He had a great fancy for the regular cap worn by the older comrades, with its attractive visor and red star.

Hu felt that, being a Red Army man, he was entitled to a cap! So he made a point of pestering the political instructor for one during the Long March. Although rather advanced in age and in bad health, the political instructor had a mild temper. He looked upon the little fighter as a child, and whenever the latter reminded him about a cap, he would laugh and say he would issue one to him later. Actually he could not keep his promise, for they did not have even a spare strip of cloth, least of all a spare cap!

The troops were continually on the move. Despite the fact that there was a lack of food and health in general was bad, they kept marching. One day, when the troops were about to tackle another snow-capped mountain, Hu felt he couldn't move a step. Having gone two days without food, he was desperately weak with hunger. His shoes were worn out and his legs swollen. Sitting on the snow and staring at the mountain before him, the top of which rose beyond view, he panted and was unable to rise. Thinking it was the end, he burst into tears.

At that moment the political instructor came forward. He had aged considerably in the last few days, with sunken features, high cheekbones and stubbly beard. His face was pale and emaciated. As he walked, he panted in a distressing manner. It was obvious that, weak as he had always been, he was now at a very low ebb. But he always looked composed and never complained of being tired. Now he stopped beside Hu.

"Oh, it's you! Why are you crying?"

"Political Instructor, I'm so hungry and I can't walk."

Sitting down beside Hu, the political instructor massaged his leg. Then he fished out from his pocket his last piece of boiled ox-hide and offered it to Hu. At first Hu declined, being aware that the political instructor had eaten nothing himself for the past two days. But the political instructor insisted that Hu take it and he was at last obliged to accept it. He felt a tremendous love surge through him.

Eating the ox-hide, Hu listened to the

THE RED ARMY CAP continued

political instructor. One must not sit here, the political instructor was saying; if he did, he would die. The revolution was hard, but it was for the happiness of all the Chinese people, so we must make every effort to play our part in it.

Now Hu felt warmer and his strength returned. The political instructor pulled him to his feet and helped him along.

Next day, when it was getting dark, snow came down in big flakes. Hu was trudging along, laboriously pulling his legs, step by step, from the deep snow. Breathing was difficult. He really wanted to lie down and rest. But he didn't dare, remembering the political instructor's words.

Then he saw ahead of him a man lying on the snow. As he came near, he realized it was the political instructor! Greatly upset, Hu hurried to him. The political instructor looked as white as the snow and was already at his last gasp.

Recognizing Hu, the political instructor said brokenly, "Never mind me … go on … don't fall out …"

Hu crouched silently in front of the political instructor. The latter took off his cap.

"Tung-sheng …" he said softly, "the Red Army cap … take it …"

Noticing the dilapidated shoes on Hu's feet, he pointed to his own, still in fairly good condition, and said, "Shoes … mine … put them on … I am no more."

The last words struck Hu like a dagger thrust into his heart. He checked himself with great effort and held back his tears. He could not accept the cap or the shoes. How could he take shoes from the feet of his leader and comrade-in-arms—even though he stood in great need of them?

Seeing that Hu would not take the shoes, the political instructor said, "Go on … go on … go on …"

It was all he was capable of uttering. It sounded like a command. His voice became weaker and weaker, until finally it became inaudible.

The wind howled madly, the snow thickened. When Hu woke from his stupor, the political instructor's body was already cold and stiff. Only then did he realize the full significance of the political instructor's words: he must "go on"!

Hu stood up abruptly, broke some branches from a shrub at the side of the path and placed them over the political instructor; then he put the cap on his head, carefully took the cloth shoes from the political instructor's feet and put them on his own, then walked on with a determined air, braving the wind and snow. Tears streamed down his face, like floodwaters in a mountain stream.

For the first time, Hu had put on his Red Army cap—the same cap he had just handed me.

Squad leader Hu Tung-sheng died quietly after placing the cap in my hands. Although he didn't say much, I knew all he intended to say. More than once, I had seen the cap and heard its history. How unhappy he had felt when, the Red Army having been reorganized into the Eighth Route Army, the leadership, for the sake of solidarity in resistance to Japanese aggression, had exhorted them to set aside the Red Army cap and wear the Guomindang one.

Hu had obeyed, of course, but for a long time he chafed inwardly. He had wrapped the cap in oiled paper and put it in a bundle, which he placed in his pillow. When a battle was on, he carried it with him. He often took it out and looked at it, and told us what the political instructor had said to him.

So I knew what the squad leader wanted to say was this: Be with the revolution everlasting. Don't fall out; keep on! Live and die for it, like the old political instructor. Be loyal, as he had been, to the revolution; give all, including one's life if need be, for the revolution.

DIGITAL FEATURE:

Images, Videos and Songs

This book includes wonderful digital content that can be unlocked using a free iPhone and iPad app. Browse through a gallery of images from the photoshoot, travel with the survey team on the Long March route and listen to Long March songs. Download your free app at *www.longmarchbook.com* to activate this content using the three images below.

THE SURVEY TRIP

Share some of the experiences of our survey team with photos and videos from their 35-day trek.

RICHARD MCLAREN

HIDDEN PICTURES

Discover more images from the photoshoot in our photogallery.

RICHARD MCLAREN

LONG MARCH SONGS

Enjoy a selection of traditional Long March songs.

LIANG DAMING

INDEX

Page numbers in *italics* refer to photographs and illustrations

ACKNOWLEDGMENTS

The publishers would like to thank the following organizations and people for their dedication, help, and support in the preparation of this book:

Organizations

State Council Information Office of the People's Republic of China, General Administration of Press and Publication of the People's Republic of China, Ministry of Culture of the People's Republic of China, China National Museum, China Radio International, Chinese Photographers Association, Publicity Department of Shandong Provincial Party Committee, Shandong Provincial Press and Publication Bureau, Publicity Department of Qingdao Municipal Party Committee, Foreign Communication Office of Yan'an Municipal Party Committee, Communication Office of Shi Mian Party Committee, Communication Office of Min Xian Party Committee, Yan'an Revolutionary Museum, Zunyi Conference Memorial Museum, Wuqi Long March Victory Museum, Culture & Education Section, Taoranting Neighborhood Offices, Beijing, Taoranting Floor Calligraphy Association, Sina.com

Individuals

Barry Archer, Natalie Batten, Chen Rong, Chen Zhiya, Delibaer, Jill Collins, Claudia Collison, Dong Kai, Du Huijun, Rachelle Edouard-Betsy, Timothy Evans, Feng Zhijun, Guo Xiaohong, Hon. R.J. Hawke, Hou Xili, Alexis Keedle, Li Fasheng, Li Ming, Lou Ming, Mei Shan, John Owen, Richard Purdy, Qin Hao, Dr. Geoff Raby, Ren Jie, Lachlan Rudd, Dr. Paul Scully-Power, Pam Seaborn, Sun Zhiguang, Bijou Weldon, Cecille Weldon, Glenda Weldon, Laxmi Weldon, Alex Weltlinger, Xiao Zhongren, Michael Young, Zhang Yingjie, Zhang Yu, Zhuang Jian.

The story "The Red Army Cap" on pages 391–2 by Wang Teh-ching was previously published in Dick Wilson, *The Long March 1935*, Penguin, Harmondsworth, 1971.